LOST™

ENDANGERED SPECIES

Don't miss any of the official *Lost* books
from Hyperion!

The Lost Chronicles

And coming soon:
Lost: Secret Identity

LOST™

ENDANGERED SPECIES

CATHY HAPKA

An Original Novel Based on the Hit TV Series
Created by Jeffrey Lieber and
J.J. Abrams & Damon Lindelof

HYPERION

NEW YORK

ISBN: 0-7868-9090-8

Hyperion books are available for special promo-
tions and premiums. For details contact Michael
Rentas, Assistant Director, Inventory Operations,
Hyperion, 77 West 66th Street, 11th floor, New
York, New York 10023, or call 212-456-0133.

FIRST EDITION

10 9 8 7 6 5 4 3 2 1

LOST™

ENDANGERED SPECIES

FAITH'S EYES FELT HEAVY, as if her lids had been glued shut while she slept. Full consciousness returned slowly and she lay perfectly still, keeping her eyes closed, frustrated by the fleeting sense that something terrible had just occurred. Why could she never seem to remember her dreams? They danced away the moment her eyes opened, remaining just beyond where she could catch them again, leaving behind only a mood or a confusing snippet. . . . Try as she would to recapture the details, they always remained lost.

Becoming aware that something sharp was poking her in the back, Faith shifted her weight. Instead of the creak of her ancient bedsprings, she heard the soft crunch of leaves and twigs beneath her.

Her eyes flew open. The first thing they took in was a

flash of color—green, red, turquoise, glossy brown—feathers catching the sun and the whirring sound of a bird in flight.

Her heart jumped. Was she still dreaming? Or could that really have been a . . . ?

Before she could finish the thought, a scream of terror assailed her eardrums. A split second later she heard the unmistakable sounds of distress—screams, cries, raw voices calling desperately for help—along with other sounds she didn't recognize. For one disorienting moment her mind went blank, refusing to accept all the confusing input from her senses.

Where was she?

Then she remembered: the plane! She shuddered at the memories: the violent turbulence, the scream of the engines struggling to halt the sudden descent, the oxygen mask flopping down from the ceiling in front of her face like a plastic tentacle, the sickening feeling of the air dropping out from under her again and again as the plane plummeted earthward, sending her stomach into her throat like the world's most horrifying roller coaster.

After that things had gone black. And now what?

Faith pushed herself upright, a rough-edged stone cutting into the soft flesh of her palm. Ignoring the pain, she staggered to her feet. Her whole body felt sore and creaky and uncoordinated. So did her mind, for that matter. Feeling so uncertain gave her a sensation close to vertigo, like her whole being was teetering on the edge of panic.

She was alone in a jungle glade splashed with dappled sunlight. Lush vines coiled up through the slender trunks of unfamiliar tropical trees. Tall palms reached toward the sky, their crowns swaying in the slight breeze cutting through the humid air. The scent of honey-sweet flowers led her eye to a cluster of riotous tropical blossoms, a bright gash of color against all the green.

The scene was beautiful—almost too beautiful, like a painting done in unnaturally gaudy hues, or a dream so vivid that even in the middle of it, it was obvious that it just couldn't be true. Even the screams and the high, mechanical-sounding whining noise she guessed might be the plane's engine were muffled enough by the foliage to make them sound distorted and unreal.

Leaning against a nearby tree trunk to support her shaky limbs, Faith took a few deep breaths. When she could remember to breathe—in, out, in, out—she could sometimes head off a full-blown panic before it really took hold.

She forced her lungs to take one deep breath after another, trying to calm herself. She caught a flash of movement out of the corner of her eye. Turning her head, she saw a two-foot-long, emerald-green snake crawling along a branch only inches from her face. Its forked tongue flickered in and out as it stared at her through elliptical reptilian pupils.

Morelia viridis, she thought, identifying the snake as its sinuous body moved gracefully along the branch.

Seeing the snake made her feel suddenly calmer and more confident, like spotting a friendly face in a room full of strangers. The snake disappeared into a cluster of leaves at the end of the branch, and Faith took a few more deep breaths, trying to figure out what to do next.

Feeling a throbbing pain in her leg, she looked down at herself. Her best skirt was ripped halfway up one seam, her faux-silk blouse was streaked with mud and grime, and both her shoes were missing. There were scratches on her arms, and the pain she'd felt was coming from an ugly-looking gash in her left shin. But otherwise she seemed to be in pretty good shape considering the circumstances.

Amazing, she thought, glancing up at the patch of blue sky visible between the fronds of the trees. Had the pilot made an emergency landing in this jungle? If so, how had she ended up here, all alone?

Thinking seemed inordinately difficult at the moment, and she soon gave up on the question. Instead she looked toward the source of most of the sounds. Her heart started pounding a little faster as she heard a woman's voice shrieking in terror. As always when she saw or heard someone in distress, her first instinct was to rush forward and do anything she could to help make things better.

Still, she stood for a long moment frozen in place against the tree trunk. Her mind seemed to be moving as sluggishly as a snake being awakened from hibernation during cold weather. Deep inside, a small part of her recognized the sensation, one that struck during the most stressful times of her life. Her sister used to call them Faith's "If only" moments. *If only* this weren't happening. *If only* she could turn back time, make things happen differently. If only . . .

Somewhere in the distance, a bird let out a sharp cry. At the sound, Faith snapped out of her stupor. This was no time for one of those moments. They never did her any good at all; in fact, they usually made things worse. If she'd learned anything positive from her trip to Australia, it was that.

Once her mind was functioning again, the answer seemed obvious. She had to go toward the sounds of distress, find out what had happened, and try to help if needed. Quickly gauging the direction from which most of the screams and other noises seemed to be coming, she left the sheltered little glade and pushed her way through the surrounding foliage.

A twig snapped loudly behind her, sounding like a gunshot. Faith whirled around, startled. Standing in the dappled shade of a large tree a few yards away, her back to Faith, was a tall, slim woman with long, wavy chestnut-brown hair. She was wearing brown pants and a billowy white cotton shirt.

"Uh, hi," Faith blurted out.

The woman glanced over her shoulder, seeming as startled to encounter Faith as Faith was to encounter her. She didn't answer the greeting for a moment, standing frozen in place. Her face was smudged with dirt and her forehead dotted with sweat. She appeared to be about Faith's age, with high cheekbones and intelligent eyes.

"Hi," the stranger said at last, her voice trembling slightly.

Faith noticed that the other woman, whose back was still to her, was standing with her shoulders oddly hunched forward. She wondered if she might be clutching a broken arm against her stomach or holding a wound on her torso.

"Do you need help? Are you hurt?" Faith asked with concern.

"I'm okay."

Faith took a step toward her, still waiting for her to turn around. But the woman kept her back to Faith, watching her warily over her shoulder. Normally Faith would have taken the hint and backed off. But nothing was normal about this situation.

"Where is everyone else?" Faith asked, taking another step toward the stranger. "The plane—were you on the plane?"

The second question sounded idiotic as soon as it left her mouth. Where else would the woman have come from?

But the stranger didn't seem to notice. "The beach," she answered simply. "The others are on the beach." She jerked her head off toward the right.

Faith turned to peer that way, catching a glimpse of open sky and a distant, watery horizon through the screen of foliage. "Thanks," she said. "Should we . . ."

Her voice trailed off as she turned back around. The woman was gone.

Faith blinked, for one dizzy moment wondering if the mysterious young woman had ever really been there at all. Why had she disappeared like that the first chance she got? Why had she seemed so reluctant to turn around and face Faith? What had that look on her face meant?

Deciding the answers to those questions and more might lie on the beach the woman had mentioned, Faith turned and hurried off in the direction she had indicated. She dodged prickly tree branches, ducked clouds of swarming gnats, and pushed her way through foliage dripping with condensation. It wasn't easy going. By the time she reached the edge of the jungle, she was soaked with sweat and her feet were ripped and raw from stepping on sharp stones and other debris.

But she forgot all of that as she pushed aside one last leafy branch and stared at the scene before her.

Enormous chunks of metal were scattered in a wide swath across the broad beach—large portions of the body of the plane lying here and there in jagged pieces, as if torn end from end by an angry giant's hands. Several of the pieces were on fire, burning with the sickening stench of fumes. Debris littered the white sand as far as she could see. The enormous sweep of one ruined wing jutted into the blue sky far overhead. Smoke and fumes and fire engulfed the scene, making Faith's eyes water.

The plane had crashed. Not landed as she'd imagined, but smashed itself to bits right here on this beach. Faith just stared for a moment, trying to understand.

There were other people on the beach, too—lots of them. Staggering away from the fumes. Helping one another move to safety. Running around looking panicked. Sitting and sobbing. Frantically calling out names.

And then there were the ones who weren't moving at all.

Faith swallowed hard, overwhelmed with emotion. It was like a stronger, starker version of how she'd felt during some of those wild demonstrations outside the convention center in Sydney . . .

2

"HEY HEY, HO HO! *Tell the traitor no no no!"*

Faith stopped short in surprise when she rounded the corner onto University Avenue and saw the protesters. About two dozen strong, they were clustered in front of the main science building waving signs and pumping their fists as they chanted. It was a beautiful, sunny Midwestern afternoon and there were lots of people on the street, though few spared the small demonstration more than a curious glance as they hurried past on their way to work or class. A couple of campus police officers were leaning against the bike rack in front of the building, lazily swinging their nightsticks as they watched the protest with obvious amusement.

Faith took a tentative half step forward, wondering

what she'd missed. She had been so busy with the last round of experiments she was running for her dissertation that she hadn't even had time to read the campus newspaper for the past couple of weeks.

Noticing that several of the protesters were wearing shirts or buttons sporting the logo for a campus environmental group, she felt a flash of curiosity. Faith had taken a passionate interest in environmental causes since childhood. But she was a little too shy—and, these days, too busy with her studies—ever to take to the streets like these people were doing.

In any case, whatever they were doing out there, she realized she didn't have time to stand around trying to figure it out. It had taken her longer than expected to finish that day's undergrad tutoring session, and she was late for her scheduled meeting with her faculty adviser, Dr. Luis Arreglo. She knew he wouldn't mind, but she still hated to inconvenience him.

She headed for the science building's front steps, planning to ignore the protesters as best she could. Several of them carried signs with the same message: "ARREGLO MUST GO!" On one of the signs someone had added a crude drawing of a skull and crossbones.

Faith blinked. Maybe her eyes were playing tricks on her. After all, she was tired from long hours peering through a microscope. Because who would demonstrate against Dr. Arreglo? He was one of the most popular professors in the biology department and the main reason Faith had chosen to pursue her doctoral studies at this

particular university. The brilliant biologist and cele-
brated environmental champion, one of her childhood
idols, still seemed larger than life to her, even though
she'd known him now for more than a year.

Clutching the books she was holding more tightly
against her chest, Faith lowered her head and prepared to
push on past the demonstrators. Whatever was going on,
she was sure Dr. Arreglo could fill her in once she got
inside.

She was almost at the foot of the front steps when a
lean young man stepped directly in front of her. Stopping
short just in time to avoid a crash, she glanced up.

He stared intently into her face. A few inches taller
and maybe a year or two younger than she was, he had
wild black hair and even wilder blue eyes. His pale face
was dominated by a large, beaklike nose. A handmade
sign rested casually over one shoulder. On it, Faith read
the words "ARREGLO = DEATH."

"Excuse me," she murmured timidly, making a move
to step around him and continue on her way.

He blocked her with his lanky body. "Hey," he said.
"Where do you think you're going, beautiful?"

Torn between being confused by the unexpected com-
pliment and irritated by the intrusion into her private
business, she answered as politely as she could manage.
"Inside," she said. "At least I was trying to. I have a
meeting."

"You're not meeting with the devil by any chance,
are you?" The young man cocked his head to one side
and made little horns with his fingers, cradling his sign

in the crook of his arm. "You look too smart for that, sweetheart."

"I'm meeting with Dr. Arreglo," Faith said. "Not that it's any of your business."

"Arreglo." He spat out the name as if it were acid on his tongue. "So you're one of *them*. A polluter. An earth-raper. An anti-green, corporate-loving establishment whore."

Even though she was tempted to let it go and move on, Faith couldn't resist defending herself. "Guess again," she said. "I'm not any of those things. I'm as green as anyone around here. So is Dr. Arreglo—don't you know anything about him? He's been a really well-respected environmental advocate for thirty years."

The young man shook his head sadly. "Ah, sweetheart," he said. "All that has changed. Or haven't you heard?"

Faith knew she should just push past him. Why should she believe anything some sign-wielding stranger on the street told her? Still, she couldn't help being curious, and he obviously wanted to enlighten her.

"What do you mean?" she asked cautiously.

The young man shrugged. "Everyone knew Arreglo couldn't be totally trusted," he said. "He was always a little too willing to sell off his convictions to the highest bidder, you know? To compromise away his principles. But this one—he just cut a deal with Q Corp. I'm sure you've heard about their latest proposed travesty against nature down in South America?" Without waiting for a response, he continued. "Well, Arreglo decided that building a new chemical plant in the middle of precious rain forest land sounds like a dandy idea. Not only did he remove his formal objections to the local government, but he's actually throwing his support behind the project—he promised to help get the poison-spewing plant going as soon as possible."

"I don't think so," Faith said. She had heard of Q Corp, of course—everyone had. The international conglomerate topped every list there was of major polluters. "Dr. Arreglo would never do something like that. A plant like that is exactly the kind of thing he's always speaking out against. In fact, I think I remember him saying something about the one you're talking about a while ago— that it was a bad idea, I mean."

"A bad idea?" he repeated. "Is that what Arreglo calls displacing thousands of innocent creatures? Despoiling an untouched wilderness? A *bad idea*?" He barked out a short, humorless laugh.

Faith shook her head. "I know him—he just isn't that kind of person," she insisted. "He cares too much about the environment to ever make any deals that would really harm it."

"Maybe that used to be true, or maybe not. But no question. This time he really did it."

The young man seemed so utterly certain that Faith didn't quite dare to argue with him. Plus, she had a meeting to get to. "Well, if he did, he must have a really good reason," she said instead, trying to be diplomatic.

"Oh, I get it." The young man rolled his eyes. "So you're one of *those*. Saving the planet is just fine as long as we don't inconvenience big business, right? Well, if you ask me, there's no good reason to make a deal with the devil. When you do that, you become the devil yourself."

"Okay, then," Faith said, turning to leave. It was clear that this conversation was going nowhere fast, and she didn't have time for it.

He stopped her by grabbing her arm and leaning closer. His fingers dug into her flesh, hurting her. "Think about it, sweetheart," he said. "When it comes to the environment, compromise means catastrophe. This is a huge step backward for the movement. Thanks to this one man's weakness, thousands of innocent creatures in the Vibora Basin will die. Birds, fish, snakes . . ."

Even as she prepared to yank her arm away Faith stopped short, hit hard by the words *Vibora Basin* and *snakes*. Now, finally, she remembered more of that conversation with Arreglo.

It had happened a month or so ago, just when news of the proposed chemical plant was first hitting the media. Arreglo had mentioned it to her during one of their meetings because he knew that snakes were Faith's passion and her life's work. Several vulnerable species lived in the Vibora Basin, one of the last large-scale preserves of their shrinking habitat. If what this anonymous young protester was telling her was correct, that habitat was about to be destroyed, dooming the snakes to probable extinction in the wild.

"Wait," she said. "Are you sure about this? Because—"

"Hey!" Before she could finish the question, a pudgy girl with a green mohawk strode toward them. A handful of other protesters straggled along behind her. "Is this another Arreglo defender or something?"

Her voice sounded hostile and oddly eager, as if she were hoping Faith would fight back. Faith glanced from the girl to her companions and back again, her heart thumping faster. She hated any sort of confrontation, especially in a group situation.

"Back off, guys," the black-haired young man said, frowning at the newcomers. "Leave her alone, okay? Go on. Scram. I mean it."

As the others dispersed, Faith smiled uncertainly at him. She was grateful to him for defending her, but she couldn't stop thinking about what he'd just told her about Arreglo.

"Go on inside to your meeting, beautiful," he said, stepping aside to allow her access to the steps. "Ask Arreglo about this. You'll see."

Faith wasn't sure what to say, so she hurried past him without a word. Entering the broad, echoing lobby of the science building, she headed for the elevator, feeling a bit shaken. For one thing, she wasn't used to having strangers call her "beautiful." People had called Gayle that all the time, of course. But even though everyone always said that Faith looked just like her older sister, she was rarely complimented on her own looks. It was something she was used to; she never really thought about it anymore.

Her cheeks grew hot as she remembered the dark-haired protester's intense blue eyes. Those eyes had stared right into her, never seeming to blink, like a viper with every ounce of its being focused on its prey. Passionate as she was herself about environmental issues, she couldn't imagine being like that guy outside—marching and shouting and waving signs, arguing with perfect strangers. . . . She couldn't help being a little envious of that sort of certainty and fire.

"Afternoon, darlin'." Inside Dr. Arreglo's book-lined outer office, Faith was greeted warmly by the professor's secretary, an auburn-haired forty-year-old named Candace. "You look pale, Faithie. Those kooks outside give you a hard time?"

"Have they been out there long?" Faith asked.

Candace chuckled. "All damn day," she said. "Ran into them on my way in from lunch. Moira down in Dr. Zale's office had to smack one of 'em with her purse before they'd let her through."

Faith smiled weakly, not for the first time wishing she could be a little more like Candace and Moira and some of the other women she knew. They never seemed afraid to stand up for themselves or say exactly what they thought, no matter who was listening.

"Anyway, the boss is waiting for you," Candace went on, already returning her attention to the papers on her desk. "Said send you on in when you got here."

"Thanks." Faith headed for the frosted-glass door leading into Arreglo's inner sanctum.

When she entered, Arreglo lifted his head from his work. His cheeks crinkled behind his salt-and-pepper beard as he smiled at her across the cluttered metal desk.

"Ah, Faith," he said, his English still lightly accented despite thirty years in the United States. "There you are, my dear. I was beginning to worry."

"Sorry I'm late." Faith slid into the chair in front of the desk. "I—um, those protesters outside held me up a little."

"Ah." Arreglo sighed. He folded his hands carefully on the desk in front of him, making his tweed sleeves rustle. "Yes, they are quite angry with me, I'm afraid. They do not like my change of heart regarding the Vibora Basin project."

Faith's eyes widened. "So it's true?" she blurted out in disbelief. She realized she'd been waiting for him to laugh, to tell her those protesters were crazy. . . . "You really did cut a deal with Q Corp?"

"I suppose one could say that, yes." Arreglo leaned back in his chair and rubbed his beard, gazing at her thoughtfully. "After careful consideration, I came to the conclusion that this is the only way to make headway with the company."

"But—but the snakes! What about the animals? And the ecosystem there is so delicate, everyone says so . . ." Faith knew she was babbling, but she couldn't help it.

Arreglo sighed again. "I understand your shock, my dear. I'm still a bit shocked myself, you see. But in the real world, compromise is sometimes necessary in order to move forward. We sometimes have to do what we never thought we could to help make a change, do you see what I mean?"

Faith just stared at him, aghast. "No," she choked out at last. "I—I don't understand."

"It's rather complicated, I'm afraid," Arreglo said wearily. "Unfortunately we cannot turn back time. We cannot make this world different, no matter how much we may desire it. That leaves us no choice but to move forward and find ways to embrace pragmatism in ways that further our beliefs."

"No choice? But there's always a choice! You could choose to keep fighting, couldn't you?"

"I could indeed." Arreglo rubbed his beard. "But as Einstein once said, the definition of insanity is doing the same thing over and over again and expecting a different result. If the usual methods are not working, it is time to find new ones that may."

"You mean by dooming a whole ecosystem?" Faith clutched her hands together so tightly that her fingernails dug into the skin.

"The entire planet is itself an ecosystem, is it not? I'm thinking globally and trying to maximize any positive effect I can have."

Faith opened her mouth, trying to muster up the words that would convince him that he was making a big mistake. But she found herself speechless. He was still her idol, still made her nervous even if she disagreed with him.

Besides, why should she have to change his mind at all? He was the one who was supposed to know how the world worked and what needed to be done to fix it. Aside from her older sister, Dr. Arreglo was the person on whom she'd based most of her beliefs about nature, science, and conservationism. Now he had decided to act against all his professed beliefs, just like that, and he didn't even seem to realize it.

Horrific visions of fish and snakes and frogs choking on putrid chemical-laden sludge lodged themselves in her head, and she could feel her emotions swirling up inside her, threatening to overwhelm her. It was no good. Her whole world had just shifted on its axis, and she needed time to figure out how to handle it.

Abruptly pushing back from the desk, she stood up, fumbling with her books. "I have to go," she muttered in the general direction of the floor. She didn't dare meet his eyes. "I'm sorry."

"Oh dear." Arreglo sounded concerned. "I hope I haven't upset you too much, Faith. I'd like to discuss this with you further. When would you like to meet again?"

The answer was on her lips before she knew it. "Never," she choked out. Tears spilled out before she could stop them, adding shame to the whirlwind of bewilderment, shock, anger, and consternation coursing through her. "I mean, I think I'd better ask to be transferred to a different adviser."

"Oh, Faith!" Arreglo sounded dismayed. "I truly hope you don't mean that. You've been such a joy to advise thus far, so dedicated to learning—besides, you're already a talented researcher and I'd hate to lose your input. Please, we need to talk about this, or—"

"No, I don't think so," she mumbled, turning away so

quickly she stubbed her toe hard on the leg of her chair. The pain made her gasp a little, and she almost sat down again.

But she resisted the urge. She knew herself well enough to know that she'd better get out of there immediately if she wanted to stick by her principles. Otherwise she was far too likely to be swayed by Arreglo's grandfatherly demeanor and nice words.

She stumbled toward the door, half blinded by tears, her toe throbbing. "Good-bye," she whispered, so quietly that she was sure he couldn't hear her.

Rushing right past a startled Candace, she headed for the stairs, not wanting to wait for the ancient, creaky elevator. She felt betrayed and confused and sad and not at all sure she'd just done the right thing. She could almost hear her sister's voice chiding her gently: *Oh, Faith. Your brain works so well—so why do you always think with your heart?*

She paused in the stairwell, gulping in a few deep breaths as she stared at the peeling cement wall. *Why would he do this?* she wondered bleakly, feeling as if her whole world had just been turned upside down again. She'd only experienced this type of utterly bereft feeling twice before, and even though those other times had been much, much worse, that didn't make this time feel any better. She closed her eyes briefly, picturing Arreglo's face. For most of her adult life, she had believed they saw the world the same way . . .

Outside, the protest was still in full swing. The group was chanting something about poison and profits, but Faith hardly heard them. Her eyes had immediately found the dark-haired young man, who was still waving his sign near the steps.

He saw her right away, too. She steeled herself as he loped toward her, expecting a smirk and an "I told you so."

Instead, his eyes were solemn as he gazed down at her tearful face. "Hey, I'm sorry, sweetheart," he murmured sympathetically.

"You were right," she said tightly, doing her best to prevent another cascade of tears.

He smiled slightly and stepped closer. "I'm Oscar."

3

FAITH STEPPED OUT OF the shade of the trees onto the beach. The sand was searing hot beneath her bare feet, but she hardly noticed the extra layer of pain. There was no room for anything else as she took in the details of the horrific scene before her.

A few feet away, a woman was sobbing uncontrollably, clutching a seat cushion from the plane. A little farther down the beach, someone was helping a man with blood pouring down his side to stagger away from a burning piece of the fuselage. To her right, an anxious-looking Asian man was shouting something she couldn't understand . . .

So much suffering. Faith could hardly stand to look; the only way she could tolerate it was if she knew she was helping somehow. Still she stood paralyzed with uncertainty, not sure where to begin or even if any of these people would want her help. She continued to stare around, feeling awkward and useless.

Being shy never helped anyone get things done. She could almost hear her sister's voice in her head—Gayle must have said that a million times when Faith was a teenager. *Sometimes, sweetie, you just gotta jump in with both feet.*

A sudden explosion down the beach startled her out of her reverie. The explosion was too far away to affect her, but she stepped back instinctively, shielding her eyes as she looked over to see what had happened. An enormous chunk of now-indistinguishable metal was in flames. Bits of it were falling over the nearby area of the beach like fiery rain, sending people scattering in all directions.

"Hey! You there, young lady! Are you okay?"

Faith turned to see a ruddy-faced, athletic-looking man in his forties jogging toward her. As he reached her, the fumes seeping out of a nearby piece of wreckage drifted past, making the stranger's face shimmer and meld into an oddly familiar shape. She stared at him in astonishment. A second later the ocean breeze blew away the fumes, and the illusion was gone.

The man looked concerned. "Hey, you okay?" he said again, peering into her face. "Maybe we oughta get you away from all these gas leaks and whatnot, eh? Come on with me, missy."

Putting an arm around her shoulders, he steered her a little farther up the beach. By the time they reached the shade of a bamboo grove at the edge of the sand, Faith had regained the power of speech.

"S-sorry for staring," she stammered, realizing he probably thought she was injured or in shock. And no wonder, the way she'd been goggling at him like an idiot. "I'm fine. It's just—for a second there, you looked sort of like someone I know. My old PhD adviser."

"PhD?" The man smiled ruefully, running one hand over his thinning hair, which was black with soot and grease. "Sorry, barking up the wrong tree there, miss. I ain't exactly the intellectual type. Barely scraped my way through high school. . . . But now you mention it, maybe you remind me a little bit of someone, too."

The stranger had a down-to-earth, unassuming way about him that put her at ease despite the situation. His square-jawed face was sweaty and smeared with dirt and ash; there were a couple of shallow gashes on his chin and a nasty-looking laceration near his left ear. Now that she got a better look, he resembled Arreglo about as much as a sturdy ox resembled an intelligent but easy-living house cat.

Just then some part of the shattered plane let out a loud creak, and the man glanced briefly in that direction. "Listen, my name's George," he said briskly. "If you're really okay, maybe the two of us should dive in and try to help."

"I'm Faith." She took a deep breath, trying to steady her pounding heart. "Just tell me what you want me to do."

George glanced around, momentarily uncertain. Then his expression hardened into determination. "Luggage, Faith," he said. "That's what we should do."

"Luggage?" Faith wasn't sure she'd heard him right.

He nodded firmly. "Someone needs to start collecting up the suitcases and whatnot from the plane. You know— grab it and stow it somewhere safe before it gets burned up or taken away by the tide. That'll make it a little easier on the rescuers when they come get us. We can start a pile over there by that crooked little tree."

Faith hesitated. Somehow collecting luggage wasn't what she'd had in mind. She wanted to help save *people*, not things. "Well, okay," she said slowly, glancing toward the tree George had pointed out, which was well out of the way of the mayhem on the beach. "But maybe first we should check to see if anyone's hurt and if we can—"

"Look, I don't think so." George's voice held an edge of impatience as he cut her off before she could finish. "The kid over there with the pens told me that guy down the beach there's a doctor."

Faith tried to follow his gestures as he waved in turn toward a good-looking, dark-haired young man around Faith's age who had just hurried past them clutching several pens and then toward another man, who was leaning over the prone form of an older black woman a short distance away.

"Now, I'm not much good with the nursing and whatnot," George continued. "But I reckon I can help out in my own way. Are you with me?"

Faith was tempted to say no. What if someone bled to death or got caught in another explosion while they were gathering carry-on bags and makeup cases? George's plan just didn't seem like the best use of their time.

"Come on!" George said brusquely, already turning away to grab a slightly charred duffel bag lying nearby.

Taking a deep breath, Faith marshaled her churning thoughts. Hadn't she just decided she wasn't going to let people push her around anymore? Then she glanced at George's face. His mouth was set in a determined line, but his eyes darted here and there, seeming unwilling to rest for too long on any of the horrific sights all around them.

He probably isn't thinking straight right now, Faith realized. *And no wonder, after what just happened to all of us.* Despite his show of bravado, George had to be feeling just as anxious and frightened as any of the sobbing or screaming people wandering around the beach. The only difference was, he chose to cover it up with action. Faith's older sister had been that type of person, too— whenever she was expecting news from her doctors, Gayle had always bustled around cleaning the house from top to bottom and creating time-consuming little odd jobs for herself like organizing the attic or alphabetizing the *National Geographic* magazines in the den.

"You're right," Faith said. "Gathering up the luggage is probably a good idea. Plus we can keep an eye out for anyone who needs our help while we're working, right?"

George seemed satisfied with the compromise. "Sure, of course. Now let's go. I saw some stuff over there . . ."

Faith scurried across the hot sand in the direction he indicated, grabbing a leather briefcase half-buried in the sand a few feet away. As she dropped it by the tree, she spotted a tiny green lizard scampering across the sand. She smiled at it, thinking how much it looked like the tiny, bejeweled lizard pin Gayle had worn on her winter coat . . .

Her thoughts were interrupted by the shrill screech of metal against metal. She turned to face the beach just in time to see the huge chunk of protruding wing she'd noticed earlier sway and then collapse heavily to the ground. It landed with a crunch and a shower of sparks, and the resulting explosion caused a chain reaction of blasts and shooting flames that rocked the entire beach, sending huge pieces of wreckage flying into the air and waves of fire and heat rolling in all directions.

Even as it was happening George leaped toward Faith, pushing her behind him. The tail end of one wave of heat blew past and warmed their faces, making Faith squint.

"Thanks," she said shyly, realizing that George was shielding her with his own body. She couldn't help being touched by his selfless, paternal act. Here she was, thousands of miles from home and all alone, and a perfect stranger was trying to protect her. . . . It was a strange feeling. But nice.

George glanced at her briefly and shrugged, his gaze almost immediately wandering back out to the beach. "This whole situation is crazy. Be right back . . ." He hurried off down the beach.

Looking back at the blazing remains of the wing, Faith saw three people lying on the sand nearby where the explosion had flung them. Fortunately all three seemed to be all right. When they sat up, Faith saw that among them was the man George had pointed out a moment ago—the doctor. With him were a heavyset young man with a headful of frizzy brown curls and a pretty blond pregnant woman in a filthy tank top. All three looked dazed by their close call—Faith guessed that the wing must have come close to landing on them.

The doctor climbed to his feet almost immediately and hurried off, leaving the other two sitting on the sand looking dazed. Faith walked toward them, wanting to make sure they were all right.

"Dude," the heavy guy said before she could speak, breathing hard and staring at her with wide eyes. "Did you see that? Talk about a close one."

"Yeah, way too close," his companion added shakily, her soft voice laced with an Australian accent.

"Are you guys okay?" Faith asked, crouching beside them.

The blond woman put a hand on her protruding belly. "I'm not sure. I guess so," she said.

Faith glanced in the direction the other man had gone. "Good thing that guy warned you when he did," she said. "I heard he's a doctor. Is that right?"

The young man nodded. "Yeah, I guess so. His name's Jack." He shrugged. "They call me Hurley, by the way."

"And I'm Claire," the pregnant woman offered, one hand still resting lightly on her stomach.

"My name's Faith. It's nice to meet you."

The words sounded weirdly formal under the circumstances, even to herself, and she giggled slightly. She immediately felt terrible for laughing at such a serious time, but Hurley and Claire smiled back at her.

"This is pretty crazy, isn't it?" Claire commented,

waving one slim hand to encompass everything going on around them.

Faith nodded. She was trying to think of something else to say when she heard George calling her name. Turning, she saw him hurrying toward her.

"What are you doing?" he demanded, skidding to a stop in front of her. "I thought you were helping me gather luggage."

"I was just making sure these guys are okay," Faith said. "Claire here is pregnant . . . maybe I should stay here and help her."

George took in Claire's bulging belly. "You having any problems, young lady?" he asked her with concern. "With the baby? Contractions or whatever?"

"I was." Claire glanced over at Hurley. "But I think I'm okay now." She started to climb to her feet, wobbling a little. Hurley quickly pushed himself upright, taking her arm to steady her. "Thanks," she told him gratefully, rubbing her stomach as she straightened up.

"All right, then. This young fellow looks like he's got the situation under control." George nodded toward Hurley. "Ain't that right, sport?"

"Sure, dude." Hurley was still panting a little from exertion. "Whatever you say."

"Good." George glanced at Faith. "We'd better get back to work, then."

Faith wasn't sure how to respond. What George had just said was innocuous enough on the surface. Still, something about the way he'd said it rubbed her the

wrong way—as if he couldn't even conceive of the pos-
sibility that she might have a different opinion on how to
proceed. Maybe she was being overly sensitive, but it set
off alarms inside her head. Why was this guy she just met
already acting as if he owned her?

4

"HERE, HOLD THIS FOR a second." Without waiting for a response, Oscar shoved his sign into Faith's hand and took off. Within seconds he disappeared into the sea of noisy protesters that stretched for several blocks along the city street.

A nervous shiver passed through Faith's body. She glanced around at the strangers' faces surrounding her. It had been nearly a month since she and Oscar had met outside Arreglo's office, though it sometimes seemed like only a few minutes and at other times like a couple of years. That was thanks to Oscar. He was like a force of nature, overwhelming Faith's shyness and uncertainty with the raw strength of his personality, entwining himself around her life like a constrictor around its prey, easily swallowing her lonely existence into the warm center of his active life. After one date—a trip to the reptile house at the zoo—Oscar had told her she was the most beautiful and intriguing woman he'd ever known. After the second date, he'd suggested moving in together. While Faith was a little too cautious to go for that so soon, she had soon found herself spending far more time at his cramped, messy apartment than she did in her own sterile dorm room in Grad Hall C.

She was getting so used to spending time with him that it had started to feel strange when they weren't together—a brand-new feeling for someone who over the past few years had grown accustomed to spending most of her time alone.

So where did he rush off to in such a hurry? she wondered, craning her neck to try to see where he'd gone.

The sea of faces shifted and flowed around her, making her a bit dizzy. For a moment she thought she'd spotted Oscar's distinctive head of wild dark hair a few yards away, but then the figure turned and she saw that the hair belonged to a hugely obese, smiling woman dressed in a batik housecoat.

Faith shrugged off a flash of panic and told herself to chill out. Ever since childhood, she'd had an irrational fear of abandonment. Oscar had probably spotted a reporter and rushed off to try to get on TV, as usual. No big deal. He might be distractible, but he wasn't completely thoughtless. He would be back.

Lifting Oscar's sign in one hand and her own in the

other, Faith resumed chanting along with the people around her—"Q Corp, stay home! Leave the rain forest alone! Q Corp, stay home! Leave the rain forest alone . . ."

This protest, the fifth or sixth one she'd attended with Oscar so far, was taking place outside Q Corp's Chicago headquarters. She and Oscar had ridden up to the city on a charter bus along with several dozen others from the university. It was the first time Faith had left the campus area to protest, and this was by far the largest and rowdiest crowd she'd experienced so far. Along with the usual gang of college students and activists, Faith could see a variety of other people out there chanting and singing, from young children to high school kids to middle-aged housewife types to senior citizens with walkers or canes. The news of Q Corp's proposed new plant site had hit the news hard over the past couple of weeks, stirring up controversy everywhere.

Good, Faith thought, pausing in her chanting to catch her breath. Maybe they would actually get Q Corp's attention with this one.

"Animals are people, too—save them from the evil Q!"

She was still a little surprised by how quickly she had taken to protesting. All her life she'd been the quiet one, the girl who never spoke out or caused any trouble. When teams were picked back in grade school, Faith was the one who'd hung back behind the others and stared at the floor until her name was called. In high school, she'd quit the school newspaper when they wanted her to be a section editor and help run the story meetings. And that time her sister had dramatically confronted a neighbor about his skinny, neglected dog, ending up with her picture in the paper and a commendation from the local animal shelter, Faith was the one who'd quietly gone about nursing the poor mutt back to health and finding him a new home.

She had never minded staying behind the scenes—she preferred it that way. But this sort of thing was different. In a huge, noisy crowd, she finally felt as if she had permission to let herself go; she could jump up and down and shout out whatever was on her mind without feeling foolish or shy. When she was part of a protest, she felt accepted in a way she never had before.

Oscar always looked at her funny when she tried to explain that to him. Whether he understood or not, though, she was grateful to him for introducing her to his world—which was also her world now, or at least it was beginning to feel that way. It was incredible to be able to look around and know that she was a part of a group of people who cared about the same things she cared about so deeply. Just knowing that made her feel almost as safe as she barely remembered feeling as a small child before her parents died. She loved that feeling; so warm, so comfortable, so inclusive . . .

"Kill the capitalist pigs!" a voice shrieked piercingly nearby, shocking Faith out of her thoughts.

She winced as she glanced that way and spotted a crazy-eyed woman waving a particularly rude sign. Faith wasn't crazy about the way protesting forced her to rub elbows with the fringier zealots and radicals in the environmental movement. While she admired their passion and dedication, their extreme positions often made her uncomfortable—especially when the media acted as if all green-minded people were like that. Still, it seemed a small price to pay for getting their message across.

She stayed where she was for a while, waving both signs. When her arms began to ache from holding them up, she realized that Oscar had been gone a long time. Abandoning the signs against a nearby lamppost, she pushed her way through the crowd looking for him. The last thing she wanted was to get permanently separated from him in this crowd, which was growing as the day went on. She wasn't even sure where they were supposed to meet the charter bus later . . .

Just as she was starting to feel a few twinges of real panic, she finally spotted Oscar's familiar angular shoulders and untamed dark hair. He was standing on the curb near the corner at one end of the protest area. The crowd was thinner there, so Faith could see that he was talking to a rather seedy-looking young man with a scraggly goatee. Dodging past a handful of teenage girls doing some kind of interpretive dance and a sixtyish guy playing the banjo, she moved closer. Just as she finally reached Oscar, the goatee guy loped away and disappeared into the crowd.

"Oh, hey," Oscar greeted her. "What's the matter?"

"Nothing. Who was that guy?"

"Who?" Oscar glanced around. "Oh, you mean Z-Man? Nobody. I mean, he's just a guy I met online. We wanted to meet up here and say hi." He waved his hands in front of his face as if shooing away a bad smell, a gesture he employed whenever a subject ceased to interest him. "But listen, he just told me something interesting. You know your good buddy Arreglo?"

Faith felt the muscles in her face tense. Even though her break with Dr. Arreglo was what had brought her and Oscar together, it remained a touchy subject between them. Oscar couldn't seem to understand why Faith kept finding excuses not to join him at the daily protests in front of Arreglo's office. Sometimes she wasn't sure she understood it herself. She had done as promised and requested another adviser, but a small part of her heart couldn't seem to accept the situation and move on.

Maybe that was because she still wasn't entirely sure she'd done the right thing. What if she'd stayed to listen to Dr. Arreglo a little longer? Oscar said there was no excuse for what he'd done, but was that true?

She tried not to worry over such questions too much; for one thing, she knew that if she went back to Arreglo, Oscar would probably dump her—he'd all but threatened to do so, more than once. She assumed he was just being dramatic, but even so she definitely didn't want to risk it. Especially not now when her world seemed to be opening up for the first time in years.

Besides, she doubted the outcome would be any different even if she did try to talk things out with Arreglo again. She was no debater, especially when dealing with a subject so near to her heart. She could never seem to stop *feeling* long enough to listen and think and respond.

Regardless, she couldn't quite stop the nagging feeling that Dr. Arreglo might be disappointed in her for what had happened between them that day in his office. After a lifetime spent admiring the man, that idea was hard to take. But what choice did she have?

Oscar didn't seem to notice her consternation. "Z-Man heard that Arreglo got hired to speak at this huge, big-deal enviro conference coming up next month in Australia."

Faith already knew about the conference—the Worldwide Ecology Conference had been on Arreglo's schedule for months. But she didn't bother to tell Oscar that. She already knew him well enough to know that he tended to get irritated when interrupted.

"Wouldn't it be cool if we could go?" Oscar's eyes were bright and eager. "We could protest his talk, let that bastard Arreglo and the rest of the world know with no question that he's now environmental enemy number one. . . . Talk about a kick!"

Faith smiled weakly. "I've always wanted to visit Australia," she said, carefully sidestepping the Arreglo issue. "Conference or no conference."

He shot her a glance. "Oh, yeah," he said. "The snakes, right?"

"You know me so well," Faith said lightly. "I mean, all those venomous species—taipans, Death Adders, copperheads, Mulgas—that whole continent is like the Holy Grail to my herpetologist heart, you know?"

Even before Faith had settled on a career in herpetology, she and Gayle had always talked about saving their pennies and making the trip Down Under someday. Gayle had always wanted to get a close-up look at the exotic birds and cuddly koalas, not to mention the rugged men with their cute accents. Faith wanted to see all the unusual flora and fauna of the faraway continent—but most of all, of course, the snakes.

"So you'll go with me?" Oscar demanded, taking a step forward and grabbing her hands.

Faith shrugged. "I'd love to," she said. "But there's not a chance. We're both broke students, remember?"

He grinned at her, squeezing her hands so tight it almost hurt. "Where there's a will there's a way, baby. Where there's a will, there's a way."

5

"COME ON, DAMMIT, PULL harder!" George was red-faced and sweating as he adjusted his grip on the strap of a large suitcase protruding out from beneath what appeared to be a large chunk of the plane's engine.

Faith sighed, wiping her palms on the front of her already grimy skirt. She was exhausted. Not to mention thirsty and hot. She could almost feel her fair skin sizzling and burning under the dazzling afternoon rays of the tropical sun. The fumes still pouring out of various parts of the charred plane were making her dizzy, and it didn't help that nearly everywhere she looked she saw the burned and/or bleeding bodies of her fellow castaways. More than anything she wanted to wander back into the shade of the nearby bamboo grove and sit down for a while in hopes it would all just go away.

"Maybe we should give up on this one," she suggested as George gritted his teeth and gave another yank on the bag. "I don't think we're going to be able to budge it."

"Not with an attitude like that, we're not," he said with determination. "Now quit your bellyachin' and help me pull!"

Faith opened her mouth to argue some more, or at least protest the way he was ordering her around, but the languid tropical heat made it hard to think of what to say. Suddenly it seemed easier just to go along with him, at least for the moment. The decision made her feel like a wimp, but she compromised with herself by vowing that she would insist on taking a break after they got this bag out—they both needed a rest by now.

George stepped back a few inches and braced one work boot against a large boulder embedded in the sand behind them. Tightening her grip on the suitcase's other handle, Faith glanced down to brace her own bare foot and saw movement on the boulder's rocky surface.

"Careful!" she warned, dropping the strap and leaning closer. A small but chunky black spider with thick white markings was scuttling across the rock. She was no expert on the arachnids in this part of the world, but it looked to her like it was probably some member of the *Salticidae* family.

Hello, little friend, she thought, echoing the words Gayle had always used when a spider got in the house. Faith couldn't begin to estimate the number of spiders the two of them had escorted outside over the years.

"Huh?" George glanced around and spotted the spider

as well. He scowled. "Move aside, sweetheart," he told Faith. "I'll take care of this . . ."

He lifted one boot. With a gasp, Faith grabbed his arm and pulled him off-balance, forcing him to take a step back from the rock. "No!" she said. "Don't kill it. It's just minding its own business. It's not hurting us."

"Not yet, maybe." George chuckled slightly and shook his head. "If there's one thing I learned on my trip to Australia, sweetheart, it's that just about everything in this part of the world is poisonous. Better to take care of it before it takes care of you."

Before Faith could stop him, he lifted his foot again and stomped on the spider, squishing it flat against the rock. When he pulled back his foot, all that was left was a dark smear against the surface.

Faith stared, horrified and speechless, at what was left of the spider. The small smudge left by its guts seemed to blur and shift before her eyes, suddenly looking far too much like a puddle of blood seeping into pale carpeting . . .

She blinked the image away fiercely, but she couldn't push away the feelings of anger, loathing, grief, helplessness, and guilt swelling inside of her. If only she hadn't said anything about the little creature, George probably wouldn't have noticed it. It would still be alive, not dead because of her. If only it were ever possible to go back and change things, fix what was about to go wrong. But it wasn't. She knew that all too well, and the knowledge suddenly filled her like lead in her veins, dragging her down.

"Okay, back to work." Brushing off his hands, George grasped the suitcase again. "Ready to pull again, sweetheart?"

Overwhelmed with emotion, Faith spun on her heel and raced away down the beach. Blinded with tears, she could hardly see where she was going. She knew she was being stupid, risking puncturing her bare feet on some bit of metal or tripping over a smoking hunk of wreckage. But she had to get away before she broke down completely.

"Hey!" George's voice behind her sounded surprised. "Where are you going?"

She didn't answer or slow down. Instead she kept running until she'd put several large chunks of the fuselage and at least a dozen people between her and George. Then she glanced over her shoulder, fearing that he might try to follow her. It was only after several minutes had passed with no sign of him that she began to relax.

Now that the moment had passed, she started to feel slightly foolish. Why had she overreacted like that? True, George's act had been thoughtless and violent and completely unnecessary, and that sort of thing always bothered her. It was natural that seeing him kill that spider would upset her or make her angry—but not that it should make her completely lose it.

"Yo." A familiar voice broke into her thoughts. "It's Faith, right? Hey, you okay? You look kind of, you know, bright red."

Turning, she saw Hurley standing there staring at her. "S-sorry," she said, wiping her eyes with the back of her hand in what was probably a vain attempt to hide the fact that she'd been crying. "I'm all right. It's just . . ."

She trailed off helplessly, not sure how to explain herself. But Hurley gave a sympathetic half smile.

"You don't have to tell me, dude," he said. "We're all a little freaked right now, you know? But here—you better drink some water before you faint or something." He held out a clear plastic bottle.

For the first time she noticed that his pudgy arms were full of bottles and cans. She just stared at the one he was holding out for a moment, her brain seeming to chug along in slow motion.

He waggled the bottle at her. "It's okay," he said. "I found it—you know. In there." He jerked his head toward the largest remaining section of the body of the plane, making his curly hair bounce.

"Thanks." Accepting the bottle, Faith unscrewed the cap with trembling fingers and took a long drink from it. As soon as the water hit her throat, she realized how dehydrated she was. The water helped clear her head almost immediately, and she felt a tiny bit better. "I needed that," she told Hurley gratefully as she tried to hand back the half-drained bottle.

"Keep it," he said, waving it away.

"Thanks." Now that her brain was working again, she decided it was time to try to make herself useful—for real this time. Most of the screaming and frantic urgency of the immediate aftermath of the crash seemed to have died down, but she was sure there were still plenty of people who needed help. "Um, do you know where the doctor is?" she asked.

"You mean that dude Jack?" Hurley shrugged. "Nuh-uh. Haven't seen him for a while. Why, you feeling sick or something?"

"No, nothing like that. I was just going to see if he needed any help." Faith was no medical professional, but as a scientist she figured maybe she could be of some use.

"Oh, okay. Good luck finding him. Let me know if you need any more water, okay?" Hurley wandered off, still juggling his load of bottles and cans.

Faith moved on as well, circling the larger pieces of wreckage as she looked for the doctor. He was nowhere in sight, though she got a closer look at some of her other fellow survivors. There was a man lying under the shade of some wreckage with half of one leg ripped to bloody shreds. Someone had rigged up a tourniquet with a neck-tie, and a young woman was offering him a sip of water from a bottle like the ones Hurley was carrying around. Nearby a middle-aged woman sat on the sand clutching a necklace and staring out to sea, rocking slightly and humming to herself. Faith recognized her as the woman she'd seen Jack trying to revive right after the crash. When Faith smiled tentatively at her, pleased to see that Jack had been successful, the woman seemed not to notice. Faith moved on, taking in the sights of injured people, people digging frantically through the still-smoking wreckage, people just wandering around in a daze . . .

Faith felt increasingly helpless as she wondered what

she could possibly do to help. She was staring at a young boy holding what appeared to be a dog's leash when a dark-skinned Middle Eastern man approached her.

"Pardon, miss," he said, his voice polite yet commanding.

She stared uncertainly at him, trying to place his accent. "Yes?"

"I'm trying to organize a few people to help build some signal fires here on the beach," the man told her. "To help the rescue party spot us. They'll need to be big, so we need wood—lots of it. And anything else that will burn—leaves, twigs, dried seaweed . . ."

"Oh—okay." Faith gave him a shaky smile. "I can do that."

"Excellent." The man nodded briskly. "Bring whatever you find over there." He pointed out a spot nearby, then turned away. Almost as an afterthought, he glanced over his shoulder and added, "My name is Sayid."

"I'm Faith. Nice to meet you," Faith said, feeling silly as she realized Sayid was already striding away out of earshot. With a shrug, she glanced around. There didn't seem to be any decent fire-building material nearby, so she headed for the tree line, relieved to have something useful to do to take her mind off everything else.

By the time the sun dipped down to meet the horizon, the burning wreckage had given way to several campfires built from the fallen branches, driftwood, and dried palm leaves gathered by Faith, Sayid, and the other castaways he'd enlisted. Watching the flames shoot up from the teepee-shaped piles of wood, Faith stretched her arms and shoulders, which were sore from the afternoon's physical labor. It felt good to stand there and rest, enjoying the warmth of the fire. The air had chilled as the sun set, and a cool sea breeze tickled her sunburned face and lifted the thin hairs at her temples.

Suddenly becoming aware of a painful throbbing in her leg, she glanced down. She'd been so busy since arriving at the beach that she'd almost forgotten about the gash on her shin. But now it was making itself known, shooting fiery fingers of pain up and down her calf.

She sat down on the sand, stretching out the leg in front of her. The last scraps of her pantyhose had long since ripped away, leaving her skin exposed. Leaning forward, she squinted in the rapidly fading light to examine the wound. It had stopped bleeding quite a while ago, and for a second she thought a scab was already forming. Then she realized she was looking at a coating of dirt and sand. She poked tentatively at the gash with her fingers before realizing that probably wasn't doing her much good—her hands were filthy.

Pushing herself to her feet, she walked down to the edge of the sea. The salt water stung every cut and scrape on her legs as she waded into the surf, and she gritted her teeth against the additional pain. She bent down to rinse her hands as best she could, then used a relatively clean corner of her shirt to scrub away the grime from the main gash. That made it bleed a little more, but it already felt much better as she splashed her way back toward the dry sand.

As she left the water, she spotted Jack a little farther

up the beach. She hesitated, not sure whether she should bother him with her minor wound when he had so many more seriously injured people to worry about. *Stick up for yourself, sweetie,* her sister's voice chided in her head. *You're just as important as anyone else.* Taking a deep breath, Faith nodded to herself and headed toward the doctor.

When she reached him, Jack was bending over a man lying motionless on the sand with a large piece of shrapnel sticking out of his abdomen. The tall, high-cheekboned woman Faith had seen in the jungle just after the crash was there, too. Her wavy hair was now pulled back in a thick braid, and she was watching what Jack was doing with an intent expression. Remembering the woman's odd behavior and sudden disappearance earlier almost made Faith rethink her approach. But just then Jack glanced up and spotted her.

"Hi there," he called out. "You okay? Did you need something?"

"It's probably no big deal," Faith said. "Just my leg . . ."

Jack stepped toward her, kneeling down to examine her wound. "You got yourself a pretty good laceration here. Looks pretty clean, though—did you wash it out?"

Faith nodded. "Just now. In the ocean."

"Okay. If you can get your hands on some fresh water, you might want to rinse it off with that, too. That big guy—what's his name, Hurley?—was collecting water, I think. Fortunately I don't think you'll need stitches."

Faith noticed that he glanced back at the other woman as he said the last part, a shadow of a smile flashing across his face. The woman smiled back, making Faith feel uncomfortably out of the loop. Were they making fun of her?

"Okay," she said uncertainly. "I just wanted to check with you about it. You know—since I heard you're a doctor and all."

She felt kind of foolish even as she said it, especially when she looked at the unconscious man still lying nearby. There was blood oozing out of his ugly wound on all sides, making the flesh around the chunk of shrapnel look blackened and crusty. His breathing sounded shallow and ragged, and his face was very pale. She turned away with a shudder.

"Sorry to bother you," she added to Jack, already backing away.

"No bother." Jack's smile looked tired but genuine. "And hey, if you can find some alcohol, it wouldn't hurt to splash some of that on the wound, too. Then just keep it as clean as you can and let me know if you think it may be getting infected, okay?"

"Okay. Thanks." Faith was far too tired to think about searching the wreckage for alcohol at the moment. Besides, the pain had subsided a lot since she'd cleaned out the wound. Still, she figured the least she could do was find Hurley and ask for more water.

It didn't take long to find him. He was making his way across an open section of beach, balancing a tray of foil-wrapped packages. When he heard her request, he nodded toward a spot near the main chunk of fuselage. "Water's over there," he said. "I'm passing out food right now. Want one?"

He held out one of the packages. Faith accepted it, realizing her stomach was growling hungrily. "Thanks."

The airplane food was cold and greasy, but Faith wolfed it down as if it were a gourmet feast. When she had finished, she went in search of the water. Taking one bottle, she carefully splashed a little on her leg, then drank the rest.

After that she just sat by one of the fires, tired and not thinking much, as full darkness fell. Other survivors drifted in and out of the glowing orange circles around the fires. One of them, a tall, lean, handsome man with the beginnings of a five o'clock shadow covering his angular jaw, wandered up to Faith's fire and leaned down to light a cigarette. Then he stood there, smoking and staring fixedly into the flames.

"Hi," Faith said, summoning up the courage to make the first overture of friendship. There was no sign of rescuers yet, which meant they were probably stuck here on this beach until morning. It didn't seem like the time to let her shyness get in the way of connecting with people. "Um, my name's Faith."

"Is that right?" The man turned and stared down at her with indolent curiosity. His lips stretched slightly into a smile that looked more like a smirk. "With a name like that, your folks must have been optimists."

Faith blushed, immediately feeling like a nerdy kid

who'd just sat down at the wrong lunch table. The man took the cigarette in one hand and sent a puff of smoke spiraling into the air as he studied her face. Then he turned away and resumed staring into the fire.

"Guess we're both among the lucky ones today, Faith," he said after a moment of silence.

Faith smiled uncertainly. "Yeah, I guess so," she said. "Although it was sort of unlucky for me in a way, too—I wasn't even supposed to be on this flight. I switched onto it at the last minute when the conference I was at . . . um, went bad."

Why in the world had she said that? She instantly regretted sharing so much. The man turned and gazed at her with mild interest, his eyes gleaming darkly in the flickering firelight.

"That so?" he drawled. "So what happened?"

Before Faith could decide how to answer, her thoughts were drowned out by a deafening, roaring, crunching noise from the direction of the jungle. It sounded a little like rolling thunder, but the night sky was clear overhead—and besides, what kind of thunder started from the ground? As the sound faded, faint echoes bouncing off the tree-clad hills, there was a flurry of squawking and flapping as birds and other creatures fled before the sound—or whatever had created it. A second later there was a loud crash, followed by an echoing tonal reverberation, almost as if the mountains were moaning.

"What the hell was that?" the smoking man said, turning away from Faith to stare in the direction of the noise.

Faith couldn't answer. She'd never heard anything

like the sound before in her life. The oddly metallic undertone of it chilled her, sounding very out of place in this overwhelmingly green, natural spot.

The thunder-crunch sound came again, slightly fainter this time. By now almost everyone on the beach was staring into the jungle. Muttering a curse under his breath, Faith's companion loped off toward the edge of the beach, where several of the castaways were starting to gather.

Faith stood and followed more slowly, not at all certain she wanted to move any closer to the mysterious clamor. It was tempting to duck into one of the larger pieces of wreckage to hide from view, just in case. Instead she merely stopped well short of the main group, peering between people toward the jungle. The treetops shook as there was another loud crash and roll, and a tall palm that had been silhouetted against the moonlit sky in the cleft between two hills suddenly shivered and collapsed, disappearing as if yanked down from below.

Wrapping her arms around herself, Faith forced herself to breathe. In, out. In, out.

The shocked murmur of voices on the beach was overwhelmed by another thunderous crunching sound. This time the echo rang out longer than ever, with an aftershock of metallic timbre followed by a series of crashes. Faith's eyes widened as she glanced to the left and saw more trees going down, one after another, most of them just a few layers of jungle from the edge of the beach . . .

Wooooooo. The weird echo was back, though quieter

now. There was a final, somewhat subdued *thump*. And then all was still.

"Terrific," someone muttered from somewhere in the main group. Nobody else spoke for a long moment, and Faith had the feeling she wasn't the only one having trouble remembering to breathe.

After a couple of minutes it seemed clear that whatever they'd heard out there wasn't coming back—for the moment, at least. Trying to convince herself that there had to be a perfectly natural and normal explanation for what she'd just seen and heard, Faith wandered back toward the closest fire. Halfway there, she heard someone calling her name.

She turned to see George hurrying toward her. She hadn't encountered him since the spider incident earlier, and she wondered if he was still annoyed that she'd abandoned their little luggage-gathering project so abruptly. But he didn't seem to be thinking about that.

"Didja see that?" he demanded, glancing over his shoulder in the direction of the jungle. "What was that sound out there?"

An attractive young blond woman wearing a white miniskirt was standing nearby with her arms wrapped around herself. "I don't know," she answered George's question, wrinkling her nose with distaste. "And I don't care. I just wish the rescue boats would get here already."

"No kidding, Shannon," someone else said, sounding nervous and cranky at the same time. "Why don't you try a new tune? That one's getting old already."

Faith glanced over and saw that the speaker was the good-looking young guy who'd been running around the beach just after the crash collecting pens, of all things. He was frowning at the pretty blond.

"Shut up, Boone." The girl tossed her head and stomped off.

Looking vaguely embarrassed, the pen guy—Boone—turned back to Faith and George. "That—that commotion out there just now," he said. "What do you think it was?"

Just then Hurley, Claire, and a slightly built bearded man in a gray hoodie wandered over to join them. "Okay, you all saw that, too, right?" the bearded guy said in a British accent. "It wasn't just me?"

"Dude," Hurley said. "That was crazy!"

"I know." Claire nodded, her eyes round and anxious. "What could make a sound like that?"

George shook his head. "Well, whatever it is, enviro-girl here will probably want to declare it an endangered species and try to get some federal funding to save its habitat."

Knowing that he had to be referring to her, Faith shot him a quick look. He grinned and winked at her and she smiled weakly in return, trying to be a good sport. She could tell he was only kidding around, probably trying to lighten the mood a little, distract people from whatever-it-was out there in the jungle—and maybe trying to make up with her for what had happened earlier as well.

Even knowing that, she couldn't help feeling a little hurt and resentful about being the butt of his joke. How dare he make fun of her like that? He didn't know any-thing about her. He didn't know her past, or her hopes and dreams and beliefs, or anything else except the few bits of small talk she'd shared with him earlier. He cer-tainly didn't know how seeing innocent creatures—or people, for that matter—treated cruelly or carelessly made her heart feel all brittle and twisted, like the wreck-age lying all over the beach. He just didn't know . . .

The mysterious woman who had been sitting with Jack earlier wandered past at that moment. She looked as stunned as everyone else.

"Yo," Hurley called to her. "You heard that, right? What do you think it was?"

The woman veered toward their little group. "I heard it," she said grimly. "I don't know *what* it was I heard, but I heard it."

"Can this day possibly get any crazier?" Boone com-mented to no one in particular.

"Never say never, mate," the bearded guy said. "We could still have an earthquake. Maybe a volcano . . ."

There were scattered snorts of nervous laughter. "Don't even joke about that, man," Hurley said, casting a nervous glance toward the mountains rising out of the jungle.

The others continued to discuss the incident but Faith zoned out, still brooding over what George had said. No matter how nice and easygoing he seemed on the surface, she couldn't just forget the way he'd casually stomped on that harmless spider earlier. That had to say something about what kind of person he really was inside, didn't it? *Actions, not words,* as Gayle might have said . . .

Realizing she was staring straight into the dazzling flames, she quickly shifted her gaze toward the cool darkness of the jungle. Bright squiggles of color danced in front of her eyes, and she squinted and blinked and shook her head, trying to chase them away. Lifting both hands to her eyes, she pressed her fingers to her eyelids for a moment, then opened her eyes again.

The squiggles were still there, though fainter. Beyond them she caught a flash of movement at the edge of the tree line—not big, scary movement like the crunch of falling trees, but something much smaller and friendlier.

Blinking again, she stared into the jungle. The individual shapes of the trees at the edge of the beach were barely visible in the moonlight. Beyond, the rest of the details of the landscape faded rapidly from view in the darkness. Had she really seen the bright flutter of feathers in there somewhere?

She took a few steps toward the jungle, suddenly recalling a similar feathery glimpse soon after the crash. As soon as she left the warmth of the circle around the fire, the chilly night air wrapped itself around her, chilling her to the bone. A wave of exhaustion swept over her all at once, making her legs shake and her head pound. Whether or not she'd just seen a particular bird in the jungle, no matter how unusual a bird it might be, suddenly seemed much less important. She knew she would be lucky to fight off sleep for the few minutes it would take to find a comfortable place to lie down for the night.

Claire touched her softly on the arm. "Hey, Faith," she said as if reading her mind. "Hurley brought me some blankets from the plane. I have an extra if you need it."

Faith turned and stepped back into the welcoming glow of the fire. "Sure," she said gratefully, rubbing her eyes. She was more than ready to put this whole long, terrible day behind her. "Thanks. That would be great."

6

FAITH STRAIGHTENED UP, RUBBING her eyes and arch-
ing her back as she pushed back from the microscope.
Jotting a few notes on the pad beside her, she sighed and
glanced at the clock on the laboratory wall. Lately she
couldn't seem to work up much enthusiasm for her part-
time job at one of the university's research labs. Part of
the reason was that Oscar kept her so busy that she didn't
have much energy for anything else. She also felt guilty
for continuing to work there at all, since Dr. Arreglo had
been the one to get her the job in the first place. Still,
what else could she do? She had bills to pay . . .

"I hit pay dirt, baby!" The lab door banged open, revealing Oscar standing there with a big grin on his face.
A tall, vaguely familiar-looking guy with a thin goatee
was right behind him. Faith scanned her mind, finally rec-

ognizing the tall guy as the Internet friend she'd seen her boyfriend talking with at the Q Corp rally the previous weekend.

"Hi," she greeted Oscar, shooting Goatee Guy a shy smile. "Um, you're early. I don't get off for another hour, remember?"

Oscar made his usual impatient little waving-shooing gesture. "Never mind that, beautiful," he said. "I have big news. Huge!"

"What is it?" she asked patiently, not really expecting much. To Oscar, "big news" could mean anything from a good weather forecast for the next protest to a marathon of his favorite show on TV.

He grinned and glanced over his shoulder at the stranger before looking at Faith again. "Pack your bags, babe. We're going to Australia!"

"What?" Faith blinked, not really getting the joke.

"I got us a sponsor for the trip!" Oscar's voice rose with excitement, echoing off the bare white walls of the lab as he jumped farther into the room. "See, all we have to do is agree to picket the Australian HQ of Q Corp for a few hours and the International Animal League will shell out for our plane fare and hotel and stuff."

Faith shook her head, still trying to catch up. "The international what?"

Ignoring her question, Oscar plowed on excitedly. "Z-Man's going, too," he said, jerking a thumb toward Goatee Guy. "And a bunch of other peeps from all over the country. It's going to be awesome!"

"Um, are you sure about this?" Faith couldn't help

thinking it all sounded too good to be true. "And what's the name of the group again? I don't think I've ever heard of them. Are you sure they're legit?"

Oscar's grin faded and he glared at her. "What's your damage?" he said impatiently. "Why do you always have to question and overanalyze everything like it's one of your stupid science projects? This is good news! A chance to get involved, learn, make a difference, move forward. I thought you cared about that sort of thing . . ."

Faith could tell he was revving up for a good long rant. She didn't want to argue with him in front of Z-Man, who was still watching silently from the doorway. Besides, even after only knowing Oscar for a month, she already knew that at least half of the things he said he was going to do never seemed to happen. What harm would it do to let him enjoy his moment of excitement?

"Sorry, Oscar," she said contritely, forcing what she hoped passed for an enthusiastic smile. "You're right. It sounds like an amazing opportunity."

"That's more like it." Seeming mollified, Oscar grabbed her in a tight hug, planting a quick kiss on her forehead. "You'll see, baby. This trip is going to be so awesome . . ."

Faith kept the smile on her face as she listened to him babble on about the details of the trip. Maybe Oscar had the right approach to life, she thought mildly. It was kind of nice to dream about something you wanted to do, even when you knew there was no way it was ever going to happen . . .

"Flight attendants, prepare for landing."

Faith was startled awake by the sudden sputter of the speaker just above her seat. Turning, half-asleep, to the window beside her, she stared out at the clouds. She knew she must have been asleep for quite a while if the plane was already starting its descent into Sydney.

She blinked fuzzily as Oscar leaned toward her, the sour smell of beer wafting from his breath. "Can you believe we're really here, baby?" he murmured.

"No," she said honestly, clutching her armrests and staring straight ahead as the whine of the plane engines kicked up a notch. Her stomach jumped nervously. "I can't."

The last few weeks had been surprising, to say the least. Faith felt as if she was still trying to catch up to all that was happening.

A few minutes later the plane's landing wheels touched down on the runway. As soon as it slowed to taxiing speed, Oscar leaped out of his seat, ignoring the FASTEN SEATBELTS sign, which was still lit up. Faith remained where she was, staring down at her hands, which were folded over her own properly fastened seatbelt. She could hear Oscar chattering eagerly to the other members of their group somewhere behind her.

When she'd imagined visiting Australia someday, she'd always pictured doing it with her sister. That was impossible now, of course. But she still couldn't quite reconcile the image in her head with the reality, which was that she was here with Oscar and a bunch of . . .

Weirdos, she thought, feeling a little guilty for the

judgment. She didn't like to consider herself narrow-minded, but the other four people being sponsored by the International Animal League weren't quite what she'd been expecting.

"Come on, you gotta wake up, sleepyhead." Oscar leaned back into their seat from the aisle, smiling at her. "We're here." He gave her a quick kiss on the forehead before straightening up and scrabbling through the overhead compartment.

Blinking and glancing out the window, Faith realized that he was right. The plane was sidling up to the airport, and the seatbelt sign was off. All over the plane, people were standing and grabbing their luggage. She yawned and stretched, then stood and straightened up as best she could in the cramped seat area.

"Come on, kids." A short, stocky woman with unkempt frizzy hair and a loud voice was elbowing her way up the crowded aisle to Faith and Oscar's row. She paused and grinned at Faith, holding up one fist in salute. "Time to get out there and attack the world tyranny of capitalism, sister."

Faith smiled weakly in return, feeling embarrassed as several other passengers glanced over at them curiously. The woman, whose name was Rune, seemed to spend an awful lot of time complaining at the top of her lungs about the "world tyranny of capitalism." She also talked a lot about armed revolution against that same alleged world tyranny, which made Faith rather uneasy, especially when she'd done it in the Los Angeles airport while they were all waiting to board the flight to Australia.

Rune disappeared up the aisle as passengers started to disembark. Faith climbed out of her seat and grabbed her carry-on, then followed Oscar off the plane and through the long tunnel leading into the airport.

They found Rune waiting for them just outside the tunnel, along with an overweight young man in his twenties with a fleshy baby face known only as Junior. "Where are the others?" Rune demanded loudly, sounding impatient.

"Chill. They'll be here in a sec."

Faith couldn't help noticing that Oscar spoke to these strangers as if he'd known them for years. It was amazing how quickly they'd all bonded. As far as she knew, he hadn't met any of them before meeting up at LAX— well, aside from Z-Man, who was one of the people still on the plane.

I guess Oscar's a little like Gayle that way, Faith thought with a sharp pang of melancholy. *She never met a stranger, either.*

"Ta da! Here we are, yo. Let's get this party started." A lean, fiftyish white guy with a long brown ponytail and a full gray beard leaped out of the end of the tunnel, splaying his arms dramatically. Known simply as Mo— none of these people seemed to use last names as far as Faith could tell—he looked and dressed like a hippie throwback, though he usually talked more like a particularly foul-mouthed gang member.

Z-Man followed more slowly, dragging a wheeled duffel bag that looked way too big to be a carry-on. As usual he was silent, his eyes darting from face to face as he joined the group.

Faith forced a tired smile as the others started chattering eagerly about the flight and the coming visit. Through her haze of weariness, she found herself wondering if she and Oscar were going to have to spend all their time in Sydney with their new "friends."

After a moment she realized that the others' conversation had turned to Arreglo—a topic that made her very uncomfortable every time it came up, as it seemed to do frequently. At the moment they seemed to be inventing insulting names to shout at him during his speeches.

"What about Planet-Raper?" Rune suggested, her loud voice bringing a few inquisitive glances from passersby.

Junior let out a short laugh, making his double chin jiggle. He said something in response to Rune, but as usual his voice was so soft and rapid that Faith couldn't quite follow it.

"Good one, man." Mo grinned and high-fived him.

"Or wait, I've got a better one," Rune put in eagerly. "Jungle Jerkweed."

Oscar laughed. "I like. Or how about Wishy Washy Wuss."

Z-Man finally spoke up. "I prefer Killer," he said in his calm, controlled voice. "Simple and accurate."

"Call him whatever you want, yo," Mo declared. "Me, I'll just call him . . ."

Faith winced as the older man launched into a string of curse words that would have made a rap artist blush. She was amazed at the depth of her companions' hostility toward Arreglo. Was what he'd done really that bad?

Maybe it was, she thought, once again remembering the

helpless snakes that would lose their only home because of what he'd done. Then again, he was only human . . .

"Okay, enough standing around." Rune abruptly clapped her hands and then turned toward the exit. "Let's go find our ride."

Faith was surprised and relieved when she spotted the woman holding a cardboard sign reading "IAL SPONSOREES." She wasn't sure what she'd been expecting their host to be like, but it certainly wasn't this pleasant-looking, middle-aged woman with laugh lines around her eyes and short-cropped blond hair. With her intelligent eyes and sporty, conservative clothes, she could have passed easily for a professor in the Bio department back home.

"G'day, all," the woman said cheerfully, stepping forward to meet them. She had an amiable voice with a strong Aussie accent. "Let me guess—you must be the mob of greenies I'm looking for."

Faith was a little embarrassed. Were they really that easy to spot?

"You must be Faith." The woman smiled at her warmly. "I'm Tammy. Welcome to Oz, my dear."

Faith smiled back shyly, surprised that the woman knew her name. "Nice to meet you," she said. "Thanks for coming to pick us up."

Led by Tammy, they all went to pick up their luggage and then walked out to the van waiting to take them to their hotel. Faith and Oscar ended up in the backseat.

Oscar slid one arm around her as the van bounced out of the airport parking lot. "Isn't this cool, baby?" he whispered, his breath tickling her ear. "We're going to have the time of our lives this week."

That made Faith feel better, too. She had started to wonder if he even remembered she was there. "Uh-huh," she agreed softly, finally beginning to believe it might be true.

"You're finally going to see all those cool poisonous snakes in person," he murmured dreamily, squeezing her tightly. "Make your dreams come true. And we'll both get the chance to make a difference in the world. A big difference. This trip will change our lives, you'll see . . ."

7

"HEY, LADY. HAVE YOU seen a dog around here any-where?"

Faith glanced up from poking at the embers of one of the smaller signal fires, which was sputtering and threat-ening to die out. Squinting in the strong morning sun-shine, she saw a boy of about nine or ten standing in front of her. She'd noticed him the previous day—he appeared to be the only child among the survivors. She had been concerned when she first saw him, but to her relief she'd soon realized he was being carefully watched over by a kind-faced man who she assumed was his father.

The father was nowhere in sight at the moment, though. Faith smiled at the boy. "Sorry, I haven't seen a dog," she said. "But I'll let you know if I do. By the way, my name's Faith. What's yours?"

"Walt. My dog's name is Vincent." The boy held up the red nylon leash he was clutching in one hand. "He was on the plane—you know, in the cargo hold. But I can't find him. He's a yellow lab, about this big . . ." He moved his hands to indicate a vaguely lab-shaped dimension.

"Sorry," Faith said again. "I'm sure he'll turn up soon."

She winced as soon as the words left her mouth. Why had she said that? Chances were that Vincent would *not* turn up soon—or at all. As a child, she'd hated it when well-meaning grown-ups lied to her about important matters like life and death. Then again, she'd also kind of hated it when someone—usually Gayle—filled her in on the hard, cold facts . . .

Realizing that Walt was speaking again, she snapped back to attention. "Sorry, what was that?" she asked.

Walt shrugged, passing the leash from hand to hand. "I said, I bet Vincent could help those guys find the cockpit," he said. "That's where they are now, you know. They left a while ago."

"Which guys? You mean someone went out to look for the rest of the plane?" Faith shot a quick glance at the closest bits of wreckage, which looked somehow even more tragic in the cheery light of morning.

"That's what I just said, right?" Walt sounded a little impatient with her this time. "Charlie went, and that lady Kate, and what's-his-name, the doctor guy."

"You mean Jack?" Faith wasn't sure who Charlie and Kate were—she only knew the names of a handful of her fellow survivors—but she felt somewhat alarmed to hear that Jack might have gone off searching for more wreckage. After what they'd heard last night, was it really a good idea for their only doctor to go gallivanting off through the jungle? What if he didn't make it back? Where would that leave the guy with half the skin and flesh scraped off his leg, or hugely pregnant Claire, or that unconscious man with the shrapnel in his side, or any of at least half a dozen others who desperately needed the doctor's care and expertise?

"Yeah, right. Jack." Walt was clearly losing interest in the conversation. "Okay, well, I'm going to go keep looking for Vincent."

"Okay." Faith barely noticed as the boy wandered off. She'd just heard the low rumble of thunder—real thunder, not the mysterious clanging, crunching, echoing kind from last night—rolling toward the beach from out over the ocean. She glanced that way and saw heavy clouds gathering just over the horizon. The sea breeze picked up, sending the clouds scudding toward the beach.

Moments later the rain came sheeting down as if someone had abruptly turned on a faucet. All over the beach, people shrieked and scurried for cover under bits of wreckage or anywhere else they could find shelter.

"Faith! Over here!"

Turning and squinting through the raindrops pelting her face, Faith saw George gesturing at her from beneath a large, overhanging shard of metal. She shielded her face with her hands and ran toward him.

Just as she reached the makeshift shelter, she heard George curse under his breath and breathe in sharply. "What's wrong?" she asked breathlessly.

George was staring across the beach toward the tree line. "Just what we need," he muttered.

Faith's heart skipped a beat. Following George's gaze, she saw that once again the trees were swaying and bending. The mysterious sounds were back, too. Faith thought of Jack and the others wandering around out there somewhere and shivered with dread.

"What kind of a place is this?" she whispered, so quietly that the words were lost in the sound of the pounding rain.

She wasn't sure how long she stood there staring toward the jungle even after the sounds faded. But eventually the rain tapered off, then finally stopped just as abruptly as it started.

Within minutes the last of the clouds rolled off over the horizon, leaving behind a breezy, beautiful day. Bright sunshine quickly warmed the damp air and began to dry the puddles dotting the beach.

Faith finished wringing the rainwater out of the hem of her blouse, then glanced around the beach looking for something to do. People were milling around, mostly in twos and threes. The exception was a middle-aged balding man sitting at the edge of the surf staring out over the sea. She'd noticed him a couple of times before because he always seemed to be alone, a little apart from the group, just like her.

Leaving him to his solitary contemplation, she wandered up the beach. A pair of young women were strolling and chatting. A man hurried off carrying a suitcase. Sayid was adding more wood to one of the signal fires, while the cigarette-smoking guy from the previous night—Claire had told Faith his name was Sawyer—lay in the shade nearby watching him. Claire was sitting in the sun on the flattest part of the beach, her pregnant belly looking round and uncomfortable. Right beside her, clad in a skimpy bikini, was the other blonde—the one the pen guy, Boone, had referred to as Shannon the night before at the fire.

As she turned away from the two women, Faith noticed George and Boone and a couple of people she didn't know digging through George's luggage collection, which they'd moved down to the middle of the beach. She stared at George as he pulled out a nylon windbreaker and hung it on a handy piece of wreckage. After a night's sleep, she felt a bit guilty about the way she'd been thinking about him. Maybe she'd overreacted to the spider thing yesterday—not everyone treated spiders as friends the way Gayle had taught her to do. A lot of people were scared to death of them. Perhaps George deserved the benefit of the doubt, even after what he'd done. Because despite everything, he still felt like the closest thing she had to a friend in this strange, scary place.

She wandered over to him. "Hey," she spoke up shyly. "Um, do you guys need some help?"

George straightened up, squinting at her as he mopped the sweat off his brow with one arm. "Sure, sweetheart," he said. "This young fella and I and those folks over there are just sorting through some of the luggage we've been collecting."

Boone glanced up from going through a leather duffel

bag and nodded. "We're looking for anything that might be useful," he added. "Clothes, shoes, medicine . . ."

Faith nodded. "Good idea." She scanned the pile of bags, hoping to spot her own green canvas suitcase. But it was nowhere in sight.

"Here." One of the other helpers, an older woman with reddish brown hair, held out a pair of white Keds. "It looks like you need these. They should be about your size, I think."

For a second Faith recoiled, wondering if the shoes belonged to someone on the beach—or to one of the bodies in the fuselage. But the woman was smiling and shoving them toward her, clearly expecting her to take them. Reluctantly, Faith accepted the shoes. The stranger was right—she needed them. Her bare feet were blistered and cut, and every step she took on the debris-littered beach risked a nasty puncture wound.

She sat down on the sand and pulled on the sneakers. They were about half a size too big, but she figured that was close enough.

"Thanks," she told the woman.

"Yo, guys!" Hurley jogged over to join them, huffing and puffing from the exertion. "Hey, Faith, there you are. I was looking for you."

"For me?" Faith was surprised as she glanced up from tying the sneakers.

"Yeah. I heard you're into, like, tree-hugging and stuff. Right?"

Faith was surprised by the question. She had spoken to Hurley several times since meeting him after the explosion the day before, but they hadn't discussed much beyond their current situation.

"Yep, she's the one for that stuff," George spoke up, pausing as he walked by with an armful of shirts.

Faith blushed, belatedly realizing who must have told Hurley about her. The afternoon before, soon after they'd started gathering luggage together, George had asked about her PhD and Faith had told him a little more about her background. He'd also made that joke about her at the fire last night when Hurley was standing nearby.

"I guess you could say that," she replied cautiously to Hurley's question as George moved on. It made her feel funny to know that people might be talking about her behind her back. "Um, why?"

"Well, you probably know, like, which plants in the jungle are safe to eat and stuff, right?" Hurley shrugged. "I don't know if you've noticed, but our food supply is already looking kind of, you know, pathetic. I figured someone like you could help us find more stuff to eat."

"Sure, I guess. My specialty is reptiles and amphibians, though, not plants." Seeing Hurley's face fall, she quickly added, "But I know a little about botany, too. I'll definitely do what I can. You know, if it becomes necessary." She was sure they would be rescued long before they had to resort to subsisting on the local vegetation. Probably today. But she was glad to be able to make Hurley feel a little better in the meantime.

"Cool," Hurley said, his smile lighting up his whole face.

"Hey, guys!" a new voice interrupted them. Glancing

over her shoulder, Faith saw Walt's father hurrying over to them. He quickly introduced himself as Michael. "Have any of you seen my boy?" he asked anxiously. "Name's Walt, he's about yea high . . ." He held up one hand to indicate the boy's height.

"Sorry, dude, haven't seen him," Hurley said, as Boone and George wandered over and shrugged.

"I saw Walt a while ago," Faith spoke up. "Before it rained. He was looking for his dog."

Michael sighed. "Shoot, he still hasn't given up on that?" he grumbled. "Well, he hasn't been missing quite that long—he was with me during the rainstorm. Guess I must have lost track of him afterward."

As Michael moved on, Faith glanced at the others, feeling concerned. "I hope Walt didn't go into the jungle looking for his dog," she said. "If he did . . ."

"Dude." Hurley shook his head slowly. "Don't even think that."

Faith could tell he was thinking about those mysterious sounds, too. "Do you think we should help him search for a while? We could check in the jungle . . ."

Hurley shrugged uncertainly. But George gave a brisk nod.

"Faith's right," he said. "If young Walt is wandering around out in the jungle, we should help his father track him down and bring him back." Catching Faith's surprised look, he smiled briefly. "I'm a father, too," he said. "Besides, we can look for more luggage while we're in there. Two birds with one stone and all that."

While the red-haired woman and a couple of others

stayed behind to continue sorting through the luggage, Faith, George, Boone, and Hurley headed for the tree line. "Michael was heading thataway, down toward the water," George said briskly. "So let's us go this way." He pointed across the beach to a spot where tall, slender bamboo stalks nodded out over the sand.

The shade of the bamboo grove felt refreshing after the blazing sun on the beach. Faith followed the men as they tromped along some kind of animal trail, calling out Walt's name every few yards.

They'd been searching for about ten minutes when Faith spotted a small red suitcase half-hidden in the leaf litter a few yards off the path. She hurried over to grab it. As she straightened up with the bag in one hand, she barely caught a flutter of movement just above. Glancing up, she gasped so loudly that the others heard her and stopped.

"What is it?" George asked worriedly, pushing his way through the limber bamboo stalks toward her. "Faith? Are you okay?"

Faith whirled around, trying to follow the bird's motion. But it was just a little too quick for her as it darted into the treetops and disappeared. "That bird," she exclaimed, still searching vainly for another glimpse. "I think I saw it yesterday . . ."

By this time the others had joined them. "Dude," Hurley commented. "Did you just see a rescue plane or something? You look way excited."

"No, nothing like that," Faith said, slightly breathless with wonder. "Even better! I think I just spotted a *Psephotus pulcherrimus*—a Paradise Parrot!"

The three men traded dubious glances. "Um, okay," Hurley said. "And that's exciting exactly why?"

Faith giggled at the confused expression on his face, feeling rather giddy. "Paradise Parrots have been considered extinct since the 1920s," she explained. "If there's really one living here—well, this is huge news!"

"Yeah," Boone said slowly. "If you say so, I guess. Um, no offense though, but are you sure? There must be thousands of kinds of parrots, and a lot of them probably look a lot alike . . ."

"I'm sure," Faith assured him. "Well, pretty sure. I mean, I only got a quick look at it. But my sister collected old prints of extinct species. She had a framed picture of a Paradise Parrot on her bathroom wall for years; I know every feather on its body. If I could get a better look, I know I could identify it for certain."

Every inch of her body was quivering with excitement. Could there really be living Paradise Parrots here? "I guess this proves we must definitely be on an island, like someone was saying last night," she said distractedly, once again searching the treetops for another sighting. "That's the only way it could stay here undiscovered for so long. I think I saw which direction it went—maybe if I hurry, I can catch up and get a better look . . ."

"Wait." Boone put a hand on her shoulder as she was about to take off through the grove. "I'm not sure that's such a hot idea."

Hurley nodded vigorously. "Yeah," he said with a shudder. "You don't want to run into—you know."

"Besides, who cares about some stupid bird?" George added, sounding impatient. "We have more important things to think about right now."

Still lost in her own wonder at what she'd just seen, Faith could only stare at him in astonishment. Hadn't George heard a word she'd said? Despite all their current problems, nothing could be more important than finding out if that was really a Paradise Parrot she'd seen.

"You don't understand," she said urgently. "Everyone thinks this species has been gone for years. Don't you realize what it means if we actually find one living here?" She searched her mind for the words to explain it to him. "It's like a chance to recover something everyone thought was lost forever, something special . . ."

"Get real." George rolled his eyes. "Pretty birds are nice and all. But people come first."

"Whatever." Boone sounded impatient. "This really isn't worth arguing about right now, guys. The most important thing is staying alive until we get rescued, right?" He shot Faith a slightly apologetic smile. "Otherwise nobody will ever know about your rare bird anyway."

George was glaring at Faith, hardly seeming to notice what Boone had said. "You know, if tree-huggers like you spent a little less time worrying about saving every last bird, bug, and lizard, maybe you could help solve a few of the world's real problems instead."

"Listen, guys," Hurley broke in tentatively. "Maybe we should—"

Faith barely heard him. "Are you kidding?" she cried,

astounded by George's attitude. "Most of the world's 'real' problems have *everything* to do with tree-hugging. We're all part of this planet, you know, and—"

He didn't let her finish. "Yeah, yeah," he said, kicking at a small bamboo sapling. "One big green world; I've heard it all before, and I ain't convinced. Didn't you people ever hear of a little thing called survival of the fittest? Huh? Why should we waste everyone's time and money protecting critters that can't make it on their own? That's going against nature's way, if you ask me."

Faith's hands flew up to her cheeks as she struggled to find the words to respond. She had heard similar arguments before, and she always found herself bewildered and frustrated by them. Did George really believe what he'd just said? Could he really think it was all that simple?

Survival of the fittest? she thought, tears threatening behind her eyes as Gayle's face popped into her head. *I suppose he also thinks the same way about sick people . . .*

"Anyway, gotta say I'm disappointed." George seemed unaware of just how upset she was getting. "I never would've pegged you as a radical. You seem too damn smart for that, sweetheart."

"I'm not a radical," Faith protested, but her voice was weak and she knew there was no point in arguing any longer. George didn't really know anything about her, and she was starting to think he wasn't interested in learning. "Okay, fine. Let's just keep looking for Walt then, all right?"

"That's more like it." George sounded satisfied.

"Come on, this way. Walt! Walt? You out there, buddy?" He tromped off through the grove.

The others didn't say much as they followed. Faith drifted after them, alternating between euphoria at what she'd seen and guilt for giving up on it so quickly in the face of George's arguments. Hadn't she learned her lesson about that by now?

But it was no use. She'd never been much of a debater; under pressure, her emotions were far too quick to take over her brain. That was one reason she'd always shied away from confrontation . . .

8

"DR. ARREGLO WILL NOW take a few questions."

"I've got a question for the bastard!"

Faith winced as she recognized Mo's gruff voice. He was leaping up and down nearby, shouting out and waving his arms.

"How can he live with himself?" he yelled. "That's my question!"

All throughout the sizable crowd that had gathered to watch Dr. Arreglo's first public press conference in Australia, people were craning their necks to catch a glimpse of Mo. Faith could almost feel the curious eyes latching onto her little group of weirdos. Embarrassed to be seen with them, she sidled over to hide herself behind Oscar, glad that the two of them had been temporarily separated from the others by a couple of overweight men in business suits. Of course, it didn't help that Oscar was now jabbing both index fingers toward the stage and shouting, "Arrest that man for crimes against nature!"

Faith glanced up toward the steps of the convention center, which were serving as the stage for this press event. From this distance Dr. Arreglo looked like a speck up there, surrounded by convention sponsors, security guards, and media types. Even so, Faith found herself unreasonably worried that he would glance out into the crowd gathered in the street below and recognize her. She was starting to wish she could just go back in time and figure out a way to avoid this whole trip.

"Arreglo sucks!" someone shouted closer to the back of the crowd.

There were a few ragged cheers. Rune, who was perched rather precariously on Junior's broad shoulders, pumped her fist. "Right on!" she screamed with all of her considerable lung power. "Fight the power!"

Faith glanced around, feeling anxious. Clearly her companions weren't the only protesters at the press conference. The crowd murmured, the noise swelling as people reacted to the confrontational comments being shouted out here and there. All of a sudden it was as if clouds had rolled in abruptly on a formerly bright, sunny day. The air felt dangerous, as if something was about to explode.

"Stop the traitor!" Rune howled.

Faith glanced up at Oscar. "Are you sure we're safe here?" she asked him, her words almost lost in the noise.

He smiled at her, though his eyes were busy roving the crowd. "Don't worry, babe," he said. "I'm sure we—"

The last part of his sentence was lost in a sudden outburst. Out of the corner of her eye, Faith barely saw something—a soda bottle, maybe?—whizzing over the heads of the crowd toward the steps.

"All right, that's enough, then!" an Australian cop shouted, wading into the crowd toward Faith's group with several of his comrades right behind him.

Faith gulped, wondering if one of her companions had thrown the object. It certainly wouldn't surprise her. At least she knew it hadn't been Oscar, since she'd been looking directly at him.

The noise from the crowd increased, and Faith glanced forward to see that Arreglo was being hurried off stage by a couple of officers. She was relieved to see that they were getting him out of there before things got any more out of hand.

"Okay, mates." One of the officers, a burly blond with a deep tan, had reached them by now. "Anyone know something about all the commotion?"

"Look out, it's the pigs!" Rune screamed.

Faith winced, wishing she could sink into the ground and disappear. How had she ended up here in this situation? She shrank back in horror as a couple of the police officers pulled Rune down from Junior's shoulders and grabbed both of them.

"Don't touch them!" Oscar cried, lurching forward.

"Wait," she hissed, grabbing him and hauling him back as he tried to push his way toward the others. "Don't do anything stupid, okay?"

She shot an anxious glance at Rune, who was struggling melodramatically against the cop holding her. Junior and Mo were yelling and fighting back, too, though Z-Man seemed to have faded away into the crowd. Oscar seemed ready to leap right in and get involved, but when Faith yanked at his arm again, more sharply this time, he shrugged and let her pull him away.

"Maybe you're right, babe," he said. "Let's get while the getting's good."

They slid through the crowd, heading for the sidewalk across the street from the convention center. As things started to thin out near the back edges of the gathering, they passed a man holding a video camera and filming a pretty female reporter as she tried to interview people.

"Excuse me!" the reporter cried in an American accent, spotting Oscar. "I'd like to ask you a few questions!"

Faith cringed, certain that Oscar was going to stop. He loved nothing more than ranting to the press at any given opportunity. Usually he didn't even wait to be asked before shouting his opinions into the nearest camera.

To her surprise, though, this time he didn't even slow down. Grabbing her by the arm, he ducked his head and dragged her abruptly off to one side, dodging the microphone the reporter was trying to shove in his face.

A moment later they rounded a corner and reached the relative quiet of the street beyond. "What's with you?" Faith asked breathlessly, leaning against a streetlight to rest. "I thought you'd want to talk to that reporter."

He waved away the question impatiently. "I'd better call Tammy," he said, fishing in his jeans pocket for his cell phone. "She can come pick us up here, and we can tell her about the others."

Faith waited while he made the call. After he hung up, his expression turned gleeful as he glanced over his shoulder toward the corner. The noise of the crowd was still faintly audible, punctuated with screams and shouting.

"So how cool was that?" he exclaimed. "Like, everyone is against Arreglo now!"

"I don't know if you can say *everyone*," Faith murmured, as usual mildly annoyed by Oscar's tendency to exaggerate.

She was taken by surprise when Oscar suddenly turned and stared directly into her face. "What about you, beautiful?" he demanded, sounding oddly urgent. "Can you see yet that we have to do whatever we can to stop him before it's too late? Whatever it takes, no holds barred?"

Faith shrugged. "I don't know," she mumbled. "Listen, do you think we should try to find the police station and—"

"Don't change the subject, babe!" Oscar sounded almost angry. "I asked you a question. Aren't you going to answer me?"

"Why does it matter what I think?" she countered, suddenly feeling put on the defensive. "I'm here, right? I'm definitely against anything that will hurt the planet. But . . ."

She was about to go on—to admit that she was starting to think that one bad decision shouldn't end a good relationship. After all, Dr. Arreglo had always been good to her, and she hadn't had that many people in her life she could count on.

Think with your brain, sweetie, not your heart, Gayle's voice reproached kindly in her mind.

Taking a deep breath, Faith knew her sister's words made sense. This wasn't the time or the place for a thoughtful, nuanced discussion on her feelings about Arreglo—especially since she wasn't even sure what they were. She and Oscar were both riled up from what had just happened; the best path was to let him wind down before trying to talk to him about anything serious.

"But what?" he demanded, obviously still waiting for the rest of her comment.

"But nothing," she said. "Sorry, guess I'm just tired or something. It's been a long day, and I'm still kind of jet-lagged."

Oscar shrugged. "There's no time for rest when the world is at stake," he chided, though he suddenly sounded more distracted than angry.

She followed his gaze and saw a familiar white van pulling up to the curb. Seeing Tammy behind the wheel, Faith guessed that she must have been waiting for their call nearby since dropping them off at the rally.

She and Oscar hurried over and climbed into the van. As soon as Oscar told her what had happened, Tammy pulled out a phone. Speaking quickly into it, she told someone to go track down the others at the local police station and bail them out if necessary. Then she hung up and turned to face her passengers.

"All right," she said briskly. "That's that. Any changes in the weather to report, Oscar?"

"Not yet," Oscar answered shortly. "Still cloudy."

Faith glanced from one to the other, feeling puzzled and left out. Why were they talking about the weather at a time like this? And what did Oscar mean, cloudy? There wasn't a cloud in the sky. Were they speaking in some kind of protester code she didn't understand?

Before she could screw up the courage to ask, Tammy turned to her with a warm smile. "Now then, Faith," she said. "Since we have a bit of time until we get the others gathered up, what say I take you to have a squizz at IAL's local bio lab? We're doing some really fantastic research there with venomous snakes—that's your area, isn't it?"

Faith was a little surprised that Tammy knew that. "Sure!" she blurted out, thrilled at the invitation. Since arriving in Australia, she'd had no chance at all to see or learn about the snakes that had lured her there in the first place. "I'd love that!"

"Good! Off we go, then."

As Tammy put the van in gear and steered out into traffic, Faith leaned back against her seat, happy about this unexpected turn of events. So far this trip to Sydney had been mostly stressful and not much fun. But being back in a lab would certainly be just the thing to help her feel more at home even in this faraway land.

9

FAITH HAD ONLY BEEN back on the beach for a few minutes when she heard George calling her name. Looking up from the bag of women's clothes she was sorting, she saw him hurrying toward her carrying a beat-up but very familiar green suitcase.

She gasped. "My bag!"

He stopped in front of her with a grin. "One of the guys just brought it in from the jungle, and I saw your name on the tag," he said breathlessly. "Thought you'd want it back right away."

"Thanks." She smiled at him uncertainly, her mind leaping immediately back to their unpleasant argument in the bamboo grove a short while earlier, and then to the spider incident the previous day.

"Hey, sorry if I upset you just now," he said with a

slightly sheepish grin, as if guessing her thoughts. "You know—about all the tree-hugging stuff? I didn't mean anything by it. I guess I can really get going sometimes. S'pose that's why my ex-wife always called me Mr. Big-mouth, you know?"

"Oh." Faith was touched by his apology. "Um, that's okay. No big deal."

That wasn't exactly true. It would take her a while to forget some of the things he'd said. But that didn't mean she couldn't forgive him, especially when he was clearly making such an effort to be nice. Maybe it was best if they just agreed to disagree and left it at that.

As George hurried off, Faith moved a short distance away from the luggage pile and set her bag on the sand. Sitting down in front of it, she clicked it open and stared at the familiar, though jumbled, contents inside. She was grateful that her books seemed to have survived the crash and the rain relatively unscathed. She grabbed a pair of sandals from beneath the books and traded them for the borrowed Keds on her feet, already feeling a little more like herself.

"What are you doing?" a voice asked from just over her left shoulder.

She glanced up and found Walt standing there. "Hey!" she exclaimed, surprised and pleased to see him. "Where'd you come from? Your dad was looking all over for you, you know."

"I know." Walt shrugged. "He found me. I was just looking for Vincent in the woods up past the inlet there."

He gestured vaguely toward one end of the beach. "I don't know why he had to make such a big deal about it—I was hardly even that far into the woods. I could still see the ocean from where I was!"

She hid a smile at the boy's expression of wounded incredulity. "I'm sure that's true," she said. "But you can't blame your dad for being worried about you. We don't know much about this place, and it could be dangerous to go off alone like that."

"I guess." Walt kneeled down on the sand, peering into her suitcase. "Wow, you're an even messier packer than I am," he commented.

"Not usually," she said. "But this time I had to pack in a hurry."

"Why?" he asked curiously.

Faith bit her lip, wishing she'd just agreed that she was a messy packer and left it at that. To distract him, she grabbed one of the books from inside her suitcase.

"Hey, you might like this," she said, trying to sound cheerful. "Check it out." Flipping it open, she showed him a glossy, full-color plate of a slender yellowish snake. "See this guy? That's a Small-scaled Snake—some people call it the Fierce Snake. It lives in Australia, and it has the most powerful venom of any snake in the whole world."

"Whoa! I didn't know that." Walt seemed suitably impressed. He pointed to another snake on the same page. "What's that one there?"

"That's a copperhead." Faith chuckled as she stared at the picture.

Walt shot her a puzzled look. "What's so funny?"

"Oh, sorry." She tapped the photo. "This just re-minded me of something my older sister did once. One year for Halloween, she glued a bunch of pennies to a hat and wore it with her normal clothes. Nobody could figure out what she was supposed to be except me."

Walt looked perplexed for a second, then his face cleared. "I get it," he said. "Pennies are copper—she was a copperhead!"

"Right!" Faith smiled at the memory.

"Your sister sounds cool," Walt declared.

"Yeah."

They were interrupted at that moment by the sound of shouting from nearby. Walt jumped up immediately and ran off to see what was happening. Faith closed the flap of her bag and left it on the sand, following the boy more slowly.

When she rounded a large piece of wreckage, the only thing she could see at first was a ring of people staring at something beyond. Then she heard a muffled grunt and a few shouts of dismay. As one of the onlookers shifted his weight, she could see a pair of men tangled in combat at the center of the circle of onlookers. To her amazement, she recognized one of the fighters as Sayid, the fire builder. The other was Sawyer—Faith had spotted him several times that day poking around in the luggage piles when he thought no one was looking, though she hadn't spoken to him since that first, uncomfortable meeting by the fire. Walt's father, Michael, was standing just inside the circle, waving his arms helplessly to try to stop the other two men from punching each other. The rest of the fighters' audience seemed content to stand there passively, as if watching a boxing match. Walt had already pushed his way to the front and was staring wide-eyed at the two men.

Faith stood there staring herself, horrified, as Sayid deftly ducked a punch and then landed a vicious jab to Sawyer's solar plexus. Sawyer doubled over for a second, then straightened up and flung a handful of sand at the other man. As Sayid turned his head to avoid the flying sand, Sawyer leaped forward and tackled him. The two of them hit the ground hard, still doing their best to pummel each other. There was a sudden flurry of movement at the far side of the circle, and a second later Jack appeared, followed by Ms. High Cheekbones and the bearded British guy from the fire last night. Jack lunged forward almost immediately.

"Hey, break it up!" he cried. "Break it up! Get off!" He grabbed Sawyer and peeled him off of Sayid. Sayid seemed ready to come after him, but Michael grabbed him before he could.

As the two men continued shouting hoarsely at each other, Faith backed away, revolted by the seemingly spontaneous eruption of violence. Why couldn't people just live and let live? She had no idea why the two men were fighting, but she was certain there was no reason good enough to excuse it. They were all in this together; why make things harder than they already were?

Deciding she'd suddenly had enough of all the togetherness of the past twenty-four hours, Faith took advantage of the distraction around the fighters to slip away. It would feel good to be by herself for a change, to relax and think without worrying about anyone else.

She skirted the edge of the jungle, moving quickly and quietly until she was out of view of the wreckage and the people on the beach. Then she slowed her step, enjoying the sound of the sea breeze rustling the leaves on one side of her and the gentle rhythm of the surf on the other. As she walked, she kept her eyes turned in toward the jungle, hoping for another chance glimpse of the Paradise Parrot.

There were plenty of birds flitting through the foliage, but none that looked anything like the one she was after. Remembering that she'd been a little farther away from the beach the other times, she took a few steps into the shade of the trees, but then stopped short. Her heart pounded as she was seized by a nearly irresistible urge to race back out to the bright, open safety of the beach.

No wonder, she assured herself. *Who wants to take the chance of running into whatever was out there making those scary noises?*

But deep down, she knew that wasn't the only reason she was afraid. For some reason, the idea of roaming too deep into all that unspoiled nature by herself made her feel anxious and wary.

She frowned at the realization. Such a feeling definitely wasn't normal for her. Some of her happiest memories of childhood involved feeling like a vital part of nature as she'd wandered all alone through the woods behind her childhood home, knowing she was lost but not really minding. As long as she could feel the dirt beneath her feet, see the sky overhead, smell the raw life flowing from the bark and the sap and the leaves all around her, she'd always known she would be all right.

No, it definitely wasn't normal for her to be scared of being alone with nature. Some things had always made her nervous, but not that . . .

10

FAITH'S STOMACH CLENCHED NERVOUSLY as Tammy turned to smile at her from the driver's seat. "Almost there," the Australian woman said cheerfully.

Faith forced a smile, trying not to let the other woman see her anxiety. She was always a little nervous about new people and places, especially when she didn't know what to expect. Staring out the van window, she wondered what the IAL lab would be like. Would it be some huge, sparkling, state-of-the-art place filled with accomplished biologists that made her feel like a local yokel?

Don't run yourself down, she thought, echoing something her sister had said to her many times. After all, she was well on her way to becoming an accomplished biologist herself. Hadn't she been accepted into one of the toughest PhD programs in the country? Hadn't she spent the past year studying under the world-famous Dr. Luis Arreglo?

She winced, reminding herself that it probably wasn't the best idea to mention that particular name . . .

"Psyched to see the snake lab?" Oscar asked, leaning over to squeeze her shoulder.

"Sure." She smiled weakly at him, not bothering to explain how she was feeling. Oscar wasn't the type of person to worry too much about anything—if anything he reveled in the new and unknown.

"Good." Oscar leaned back in his own seat, smiling at her. "I'm really glad you're getting the chance to see the important work IAL is doing for the world. They're a really fantastic group, you know. Totally dedicated to the cause of environmental conservation and stuff."

"That's right," Tammy said cheerfully as she slowed the van and took a sharp turn into a parking lot.

Faith glanced out the window again. She hadn't known what to expect, but it wasn't this rather seedy strip mall with several empty storefronts and piles of trash in the parking lot.

"Um, is this it?" she asked, trying to keep her voice neutral.

"This is it," Tammy said. "I know it doesn't look like much, but we were more concerned with the facilities than with appearances."

Feeling vaguely chastised, Faith just nodded. She climbed out of the van and followed Tammy and Oscar toward one of the plate-glass storefronts. The large windows had been blocked out with brown paper taped to the insides, but a small, computer-printed sign on the door identified the place as PRO HLTH LAB: *AUTHORISED VISITORS ONLY.*

"Pro health?" Faith whispered to Oscar as Tammy fiddled with the ring of keys she'd just pulled from her jacket pocket. "What does that mean?"

Oscar shrugged. "I don't know," he said, sounding a little impatient. "It's just what they call the place, I guess, okay?"

"Here we go," Tammy sang out, unlocking the door and standing back to usher them through.

Faith followed Oscar inside and looked around. The lab evidently had been an optometrist's office in the not-too-distant past. There were still several glass display cases here and there and a few eye charts on the walls.

Banishing a twinge of disappointment, Faith reminded herself that as Tammy had said, appearances weren't important. Besides, environmental groups rarely had the funding for large, fancy facilities the way a company like Q Corp did. That was just the way of the world.

Spotting several large glass tanks lined up on a counter at the back of the room, she smiled. "Hey," she said. "Do you have snakes in there?"

"Yeah." Tammy smiled. "Want to see? We have specimens of most of the major venomous Australian species."

"Great!" Her nerves forgotten, Faith hurried over and peered into the first of the tanks.

Oscar joined her. "Cool-looking snake," he commented. "What is it?"

"That's a *Tropidechis carinatus*, better known as a

Rough-scaled Snake," Faith told him, identifying the three-foot-long snake easily by its distinctive scales. "They don't usually produce that much venom but, unlike most snakes, they're pretty bad-tempered. More likely to fight—and bite—than flee."

"Right-o." Tammy pointed to the next tank in the line, which contained a much larger snake. "Did you see this little guy?"

Faith moved over to look. "Hey, is that a Mulga?"

As Tammy nodded, Oscar also looked into the second tank. "What's a Mulga?" he asked. "Is it poisonous, too?"

"It's a Mulga Snake, also known as a King Brown Snake, even though it's more closely related to black snakes than the browns," Faith told him. "Its venom isn't quite as toxic as some, but it has the largest output of any snake in Australia."

"Does that mean it's more dangerous than the first snake there?" he asked.

Faith was pleasantly surprised by his questions. Back home, he'd never showed much interest in the details of her work. Maybe seeing the snakes up close and personal had piqued his curiosity, or maybe he was just trying to make up for their earlier argument about Arreglo. Either way, she was more than happy to talk to him about her favorite subject.

"It's hard to say," she said. "The Mulga can become aggressive, too, but like I said, the Rough-scaled Snake is more known for attacking people. I don't know the fatality statistics offhand." She shrugged. "With modern antivenins, most snakebites aren't lethal anymore, anyway."

They moved on down the line, looking at several other snakes—a taipan, an Eastern Brown Snake, a Death Adder. Faith was thrilled by the chance to see them all up close and in one place. So what if the lab was a little shabbier than the ones back home at the university? This was why she'd agreed to this trip. For the first time since getting off the plane, she was one hundred percent glad she'd come.

Tammy seemed to be enjoying Faith's enthusiasm. "Oscar said you were a snake person," she commented. "I can see he was right. How did you get interested in something like that?"

Faith glanced at her shyly. "Well, I've always loved all sorts of animals, and especially reptiles and amphibians," she said. "My older sister got me started early—she used to love telling people how she sneaked a frog into my crib when I was just a baby." She smiled at the memory. "I guess she thought I needed a pet."

"Ah, so it's a family trait." Tammy smiled. "Is your sister a biologist, too, then?"

"No." Faith felt the familiar hollow ache in her heart that always came when she talked about Gayle. "She—um, she was a music teacher and a singer. But she died a few years ago. Cancer. She's the one who sort of inspired my research at the university—once I heard about the stuff people are doing with snake venoms, trying to find a cure for cancer, I knew it was for me. I just think it's amazing that snake venom—something that most people think of as horrible and deadly and wrong—could actually hold the key to, you know, ending that kind of pain. Once I have my degree, I want to get involved in that kind of research full-time."

Her last few words trailed off bashfully into silence. She wasn't used to talking so much about herself, especially to a virtual stranger. But Tammy seemed very interested in what she'd said.

"Oh, but that's such a coincidence!" the Australian woman exclaimed. "Didn't Oscar tell you?"

Faith glanced at Oscar, who looked blank. "Tell me what?" she asked.

"That's one of our primary areas of research here," Tammy said. "The IAL is at the forefront of such things—cancer research, snake venoms, the lot."

"Oh yeah, that's right." Oscar shrugged and grinned sheepishly. "I guess I forgot."

"Really?" Faith looked from one to the other, surprised. "That's so cool! So what kinds of experiments are you guys running right now? Do you stick with local species, or do you import venom from other countries? Have you looked into the—"

Tammy laughed, raising both hands as if to ward off the questions. "Wait, wait!" she cried. "I'm a PR specialist, not a scientist, so I don't know all the technical ins and outs of the project. Sorry. But I'll see that you get a chance to sit down with the people doing the research— we should be able to set something up once we've finally figured out a way to deal with the Arreglo crisis . . ."

"Oh, okay. That sounds good." Faith couldn't help

feeling vaguely guilty all of a sudden at the mention of Dr. Arreglo's name. It was one thing to defend him to hotheaded Oscar, who sometimes seemed to disapprove of everyone and everything besides himself. But knowing that someone like Tammy was working so hard against Arreglo as well made her feel bad for even thinking about wanting to reconcile with her adviser.

"We're back!" The lab door burst open and several people spilled in. "Did you miss us?"

It was Mo, sporting a black eye and a cocky grin. Z-Man, Junior, and Rune were right behind him.

"Mo!" Oscar hurried forward to trade high fives. "Dude, check you out! Police brutality at its finest!"

"I guess." Mo laughed. "Man, the elbows were flying so fast I don't know who got me. Mighta been this bastard here, actually." He hooked a thumb toward Junior, who grinned sheepishly.

Tammy had also left the snake tanks to greet the newcomers. "Did you have any problems at the police station?" she asked.

"Nope, Z-Man talked us out with no trouble at all," Rune replied.

Faith found that hard to believe. She'd barely heard Z-Man speak ten words in the time she'd known him so far. But he nodded serenely as Tammy thanked him for his good work.

At that point Junior began mumbling eagerly about something she couldn't quite follow. Oscar broke in with a question, and then there was a burst of chatter as all of them started talking about the press conference, the protest, and everything else that had happened.

Meanwhile Faith stayed where she was, standing forgotten by the snake tanks. The brief moment of comfort had passed and she was on the outside again, feeling alone and uncomfortable.

11

BREATHE. **FAITH FOUGHT BACK** the uncomfortable feeling of panic, forcing herself to put one foot in front of the other as she moved farther into the jungle. She'd finally grown frustrated with her own fearful feelings and decided to force herself to explore a little deeper. How else was she ever going to catch another glimpse of the Paradise Parrot, if that was really what she'd seen earlier?

Her heart thumped loudly with every step, but so far there was no sign of anything out of the ordinary. It was just a sunny, steamy, perfectly normal day in the jungle. Birds cried out overhead, broad tropical leaves waved lazily in the slight breeze, insects buzzed around here and there—there was absolutely nothing to be scared of . . .

"Aaaaaah!"

The terrified scream, coming from somewhere in the

forest nearby, evoked a startled yelp. Immediately forgetting her own fears, Faith leaped into motion, rushing toward the source of the shout. Whoever had cried out sounded terrified and desperate. In the back of her mind, it occurred to her that she could be racing right toward whatever had made those terrifying noises, but she couldn't stop. She had to help if she could.

She burst into a large, rocky clearing ringed by trees and, on one side, a bamboo grove. George was standing frozen in place beside a tumbledown pile of large, mossy boulders. He was gripping a banged-up piece of luggage which, judging by the dirt on its sides, he'd just yanked out from under one of the rocks.

"George?" Faith said uncertainly. "Was that you yelling just now?"

He didn't move a muscle as he answered through clenched teeth. "Don't make any sudden moves," he hissed. "Or it might strike."

Faith blinked, not sure what he was talking about. She felt a flash of fear as she scanned the trees around them, wondering if the monster could be lurking there waiting to leap out and pounce on them both. But aside from the gentle flapping of foliage in the breeze and the constant but nearly imperceptible sway of the tall, pliable bamboo stalks, there was no sign of movement anywhere.

It was only when she glanced back at George that she finally realized what was wrong with him. When she did, she wasn't sure whether to roll her eyes or laugh out loud. Clinging to the side of the suitcase, its tongue flicking in and out, was a slender, one-and-a-half-foot-long yellowish green snake. That was all. And yet he was clearly so scared that he couldn't move a muscle even to put down the bag and move away.

Faith took a step forward, smiling and making her voice as reassuring as possible as she spoke. "It's okay, George," she said. "That's just a baby tree python—the scientific name is *Morelia viridis*."

"P-python?" George repeated. "Those are pretty dangerous, right?"

"Not at all," Faith replied soothingly. "Trust me, it's not going to hurt you. It's nonvenomous and probably more scared of you than you are of it."

That seemed to be both the right and wrong thing to say. George finally jerked into motion, tossing the suitcase halfway across the clearing. When it hit the ground its clasp gave way and it burst open, sending clothes and toiletries flying in all directions.

"Pardon me, missy, but for your information I wasn't *scared*," he spat out, wheeling to glare at Faith. "And I don't appreciate you saying so. You don't have to be some kind of sissy coward to be cautious around a strange snake."

"Yes, I know. I—I'm sorry," she stammered, realizing he must have taken her comment as some kind of grave insult to his manhood. "I was just trying to—"

He hardly seemed to hear her. His face was red with anger as he jabbed one finger toward her. "And I really don't appreciate the superior attitude, either. Not everybody thinks like you, you know. That doesn't make you queen of the jungle or whatever the hell you think you are."

Faith took a step backward, startled and a little frightened by the fury in his eyes. "But I don't—"

"You know, people like you make me sick," he cried, still jabbing his finger at her. "You spend all your time figuring out ways to make things harder for the rest of us, and for what? You want progress to stop just to save a few stupid creatures that no one likes anyway!"

Stooping, he grabbed a stout tree branch off the ground and glared at her. Faith froze, not knowing how to react. While she would have had no trouble facing down an angry snake in striking position, she had absolutely no experience dealing with people in a similar mood.

But instead of coming toward her, he whirled around and stomped toward the fallen suitcase.

"Okay, where'd you go, you slimy little sonofabitch?" he muttered. He whacked the stick soundly against his free hand, then used it to poke at the suitcase, flipping it over. "Go ahead, I dare ya to show your ugly little head again. Then you'll see just how important an opposable thumb really is . . ."

Fortunately the snake had long since disappeared. Faith stared blankly at George for another moment as he stomped around the clearing with his weapon, then finally gathered her wits enough to turn and walk away, leaving him still ranting furiously at the absent snake.

She wandered aimlessly through the jungle for a few minutes, her earlier fears temporarily forgotten. She was shaken by the idea that some people could go from nice to nasty over something so minor. Especially when she was only trying to help . . .

Maybe I should have seen it coming, Faith told herself, thinking of the fate of that innocent spider. And it wasn't as if she was exactly a genius when it came to judging people's true characters—recent events had proven that well enough.

She shook her head, grimacing at the painful memories that immediately flashed through her mind. *Actions, not words*, as Gayle would say . . .

12

"ACTION, NOW! TELL THEM no, now!" Oscar shouted at the top of his lungs.

Beside him, Faith swallowed a sigh. So far, their picketing duty outside Q Corp's Sydney headquarters was turning out to be tedious and a little embarrassing. There were no more than two dozen protesters marching along the sidewalk outside the impressive-looking glass-and-steel building, including their little group, and only two bored-looking police officers stood nearby keeping an eye on things.

"How much longer do we have to stay here?" she whispered to Oscar when he paused for breath.

"As long as it takes," he said, switching his anti-Q sign from one hand to the other and wiping the sweat from his brow. "Until they listen to us. We can't give up."

Just then Junior wandered over, clutching a small boom box under one beefy arm. "Check it out," he said, for once his soft, quick words clear enough for Faith to understand. "I found a station playing the traitor's speech."

Faith didn't even have to ask who he meant. She had heard the others refer to Arreglo by insulting names so many times already on this trip that she was almost getting used to it. Almost.

"I don't want to hear what that sellout has to say," Oscar declared.

But the others were already gathering around Junior. "Know thy enemy, my boy," Mo said, holding up one finger for emphasis. "If we don't listen to what he has to say, how can we combat it?"

Junior set the radio on the sidewalk, sat down on the curb beside it, and turned up the volume. The others joined him, and Faith perched on the curb at one end beside Rune, relieved to have an excuse to stop walking around with her sign for a few minutes. Only Oscar remained standing, looking stubborn and irritated. But Faith could tell he was listening, too, as he hovered nearby.

". . . and I regret to say that the purpose of this conference has been overshadowed by my recent decision regarding the Vibora Basin project," Dr. Arreglo's clear, lightly accented voice poured out of the radio, just a little scratchy thanks to the cheap speakers. "Some people are criticizing me for compromising with Q Corp, and I do understand their concerns. But of those people I ask this: Is it better to take an offer to meet halfway, or hold out for a hundred-percent solution that's ninety-nine percent unlikely to happen? To me, the answer was clear. Q Corp would find a way to make this plant happen with or without me. So I decided to put aside my old distaste for this company, with their admittedly poor environmental record, and do what I could to help turn that record around, at least a little bit. After all, one can't have an influence if one isn't willing to engage."

Faith caught herself nodding slightly, realizing that what Arreglo was saying made sense. It reminded her of one of Gayle's favorite sayings: *Don't throw the baby out with the bathwater*. She glanced around at the others to see if they were thinking the same way, but she couldn't read their faces.

Meanwhile Arreglo was still talking. ". . . and pledged that a portion of the Vibora Basin rain forest will be set aside as protected land. And with the money Q Corp has promised to commit to maintaining this refuge, we can rest assured that it will be truly protected, with no danger of poachers or the other usual threats. And that, I think we can all agree, is a positive thing."

"Sellout," Oscar muttered loudly as the station cut away to a commercial.

"Yeah." Junior turned down the volume. "Sounds like a buncha excuses to me."

"Some folks'll say anything to save their own nether regions," Mo added, nodding sagely.

"The bastard!" Rune added hotly.

Oscar clenched his sign handle with both fists. "You

know, I wonder how many people will even listen to this stupid speech, or anything else he has to say from now on," he commented acidly. "After that mess of a press conference yesterday, I wonder if he'll even live through this visit to Australia." He grinned and glanced around at the others, clearly pleased with his own comment.

Faith was horrified. Hadn't they heard what Arreglo had just said? Hadn't his explanation changed their minds about him at all? It had certainly made her start to think again, to wonder if maybe she'd been looking at things the wrong way all along . . .

"How can you say that?" she blurted out. "It almost sounds like you'd be happy if something terrible happened to him."

"And you sound like an apologist for the corporate pigs," Oscar countered. "I mean, just think about all the millions of lives that could be saved if Arreglo's happened to end right now. Without his support and all the good publicity he's bringing them, I'm betting these jerks"—he paused just long enough to gesture at the edifice behind them— "might rethink their plans for the Vibora Basin."

"Fat chance," Rune muttered. "The only thing they think about is money."

Oscar ignored her. He was in full-on rant mode by now, his face red and his eyes bright with righteous indignation. "Millions of lives," he told Faith. "Think about that. Birds. Fish. Monkeys. Your precious snakes. All of them. Q Corp could build their stupid plant anywhere. But none of those creatures have a choice about where to live. It's the Vibora Basin or oblivion for them."

"I know," Faith said. "But—"

"But what?" Oscar demanded. "Arreglo's got to be stopped, that's all I'm saying here. Survival of the fittest, baby. Survival of the fittest. It's what all you biology types believe in, right? And after the way Arreglo sold out, can you blame me for not thinking it's such a bad idea to trade one guilty life for countless innocent ones?"

"Easy, brother," Z-Man murmured. "It's okay."

Oscar waved him away. "No, it's not okay," he declared. He reached out and jabbed Faith sharply in the chest with one finger. "She claims to care about animals and the health of the planet. And hey, she's a scientist— she should be able to do the basic math. Can she really not see what I'm trying to say? One life versus millions?"

"Um . . ." Trying to be fair, as well as buy herself a few seconds to gather her thoughts, Faith paused and considered what he was saying. It was true in a way. With his one decision, no matter how nuanced or strictly negotiated, Arreglo had sentenced innumerable individual creatures—snakes, birds, insects, tree frogs, mammals, and many more—to death, and probably quite a few of their species to almost certain extinction. Looked at in the hard, cold light of logic, Oscar's solution seemed simple and almost elegant. Remove the one, and the millions could continue to prosper.

"Well?" Oscar demanded impatiently.

"I can sort of see your point," she admitted softly.

Then an image of Dr. Arreglo flashed through her mind—the two of them sitting in his office, him smiling at her as they discussed biodiversity or gene mutation or just the results of the latest Bears game. She immediately realized how crazy and limited that kind of black-and-white thinking was.

"But that's not the only solution," she added quickly, even as Oscar's expression began to soften. "There are better ways to handle things. Compromise doesn't always mean selling out, you know. You heard what Dr. Arreglo said just now—he thought this would be the better solution overall. And—and I think I might trust him on that."

"What?" Oscar's face hardened again, and his voice sounded strangled.

Jutting out her chin slightly, Faith went on without pausing to think about what she was going to say. "I do, I believe him," she said defiantly. "I know he's a good man who cares about the world; I don't really know why I doubted that in the first place." She shrugged. "When we get back home, I hope he'll agree to be my adviser again."

For once, Oscar appeared speechless. He stared at her blankly, his protest sign hanging limply at his side.

"Listen, you two . . ." Rune began uncertainly, while Z-Man and Mo exchanged a worried glance and Junior stared at the ground.

"Fine," Oscar spat out at last. "I guess you're not the

person I thought you were. Now if you'll all excuse me, I'm out of here."

"Oscar, wait!" Faith cried, shocked to the core by the loathing in his face as he glared at her.

But it was too late. He spun on his heel and stormed off, almost knocking over a couple of other picketers as he left.

Faith took a few steps after him, then stopped, blinded by tears. Behind her, she could hear the others buzzing quietly about the fight, but she ignored them. She was tired of trying to fit in with these people, when the truth was, she didn't. She wasn't even sure she fit in with Oscar anymore—or with anyone, for that matter . . .

She needed to be alone—she couldn't stand to break down in front of these unsympathetic near-strangers. Mumbling some sort of excuse about finding a bathroom, Faith raced off around the corner of the building.

She spent the next few minutes sobbing behind a Dumpster. Her mind was such a whirlwind of emotion that it was hard to think straight. All she knew was that what Arreglo had said on the radio sounded rational and realistic—in other words, the exact opposite of everything Oscar had been saying lately. She just couldn't deny that any longer.

But what did that mean for their romance? It was Oscar's outspoken idealism that had brought them together. Was it now about to tear them apart? The very idea was like a knife in her heart. Being with Oscar was often challenging, but even after such a short time, she couldn't imagine going back to life without him. When he was fully focused on her, he made her feel like the only person in the world who mattered, and that was a feeling she hadn't had in a long, long time.

Finally, feeling cried out, she forced herself to leave her hiding place and head back to the others, hoping Oscar might have returned. He had a hot temper, but his fits of passion usually dissipated just as quickly as they began. They needed to talk this out as soon as possible, before it blew up into something bigger than it was. If they truly cared about each other, they would get through this. Now that she was feeling a little calmer, she was sure of it. She would forgive him for the mean names he'd called her, he would do his best to accept her change of heart about Arreglo, and they would take it from there.

As she approached the others, she saw that they were lined up on the curb with their backs to her. There was no sign of Oscar, though, and her heart sank.

The others were talking with one another, and as Faith got closer some of their words drifted toward her. ". . . and we're going to have to change the plan, no matter what the bro told us to start," Mo was saying with obvious dismay in his voice.

"I disagree," Rune said, her loud voice carrying more easily. "It can still work. All we need is the in, right?"

"She's right," Z-Man said. "If we . . ."

The rest of his comment, as well as subsequent responses by Junior and Mo, were mostly lost in the noise of passing traffic and the other picketers, who had just started another chant. Faith caught only a few brief phrases here and there: "worth the risk," "if he's still willing to go in," and "no matter how it ends up, the point is made." And then Rune's next comment: "Okay, but why not just use the whole snake?"

Faith blinked, momentarily intrigued by the odd remark. But she had more pressing things on her mind at the moment than worrying about whatever weird protesting plans those freaks were discussing now. Clearing her throat, she took another few steps toward them.

"Hey, guys," she said softly.

They spun around, and the conversation stopped abruptly. "Hey, Faith," Mo said, his voice dripping concern. "Are you okay? We were just going to come looking for you."

"Yeah," Rune added. "We called Tammy. She's on her way to pick us up."

"What about Oscar?" Faith asked uncertainly.

Z-Man shrugged. "Dude will turn up," he murmured. "He won't want to miss our ride."

Faith had her doubts, but Z-Man's prediction turned out to be right. Seconds after Tammy's familiar white van pulled up to the curb, Oscar appeared. He wandered over to the group, though he refused to meet Faith's eye.

"Are we going?" he asked sullenly.

Tammy traded a glance with Rune. "Okay, you two," she said in her brisk, no-nonsense voice. "I heard our resident lovebirds had a bit of a tiff. Now, we don't have time for that—we're all on the same side here, remember? So I want you to kiss and make up." She shot Oscar a meaningful look. "I'm sure if you think about it, Oscar, you'll realize you still *need* Faith. Right?"

It seemed like an odd way of putting things, and Faith wondered if it was some kind of Aussie slang she hadn't heard before. Regardless, it seemed to do the trick. Oscar stared at Tammy for a moment, then shrugged.

"You're right, Tammy," he said gruffly. He turned toward Faith and gave her a rather stiff smile. "Guess maybe I got a little excited or whatever. Forgive me, baby?"

"Sure, I guess," Faith squeaked, too surprised to say anything more.

"Good." Tammy clapped her hands. "All right, kids. All aboard." As they all moved toward the van, she put a hand on Oscar's arm to stop him. "A word, mate?"

The two of them traded a few whispers out on the sidewalk as Faith and the others settled themselves into their usual seats in the van. Glancing out the open door, Faith couldn't help wondering what Tammy, who seemed to be doing most of the talking, was saying. Was she chiding Oscar for being mean to her? What had the others told her on the phone, anyway? In any case, she was touched by the way the Australian woman was taking such an interest in her and their relationship.

After a moment Oscar climbed in and sat beside Faith as Tammy closed the door and walked up to the driver's seat. His smile looked more sincere this time, and he immediately looped his arm around her shoulders and leaned in to nuzzle her neck.

"I mean it, babe," he said huskily, his face so close to hers that she could smell the Italian dressing he'd had for lunch several hours earlier. "You'll forgive what I said, right? Please say yes, or I'll die—I mean it. You mean the world to me, babe. Honest. I don't know why I called you those names; I was just being a jerk, I guess."

"Don't worry about it," she whispered back, touched by his earnest tone. "We both said stupid stuff, I guess. It's no big deal."

"Great." He smiled, then kissed her.

Doing her best to push everything else out of her mind, she kissed him back until the others started whooping playfully at them. Then they both burst out laughing and pulled apart. Faith leaned back against the seat, Oscar's hand held tightly in her own, feeling tired and a little confused . . . but mostly happy.

Soon they were on the road making their way through Sydney's busy rush-hour traffic. Faith assumed they were heading back to the hotel, but after a few minutes the van turned into an almost-empty parking lot. Glancing out the window, Faith realized they had arrived at the IAL lab.

"What are we doing here?" she asked.

"Surprise." Tammy turned and smiled at her. "I figured you guys would be starving after the long afternoon of picketing. So I had dinner brought in for all of us."

The others erupted in cheers, and Faith smiled along. So far, the lab was the place she'd felt most comfortable in all of Sydney. While she'd been looking forward to talking things out in private with Oscar, she figured that could wait a while.

Soon they were all sitting around a big round table in the middle of the lab's main room, stuffing themselves with take-out food and chatting about the day's events. Faith still felt a bit uncomfortable with the group, especially whenever the talk turned to Arreglo. But she did her best to let it wash over her as she concentrated on her food.

At one point toward the end of the meal, she saw Rune get up from the table, a piece of a corn chip held between two fingers. "Here, snakey-snakey," she cooed, wandering to the back of the room and holding the chip over one of the tanks.

"Hey!" Faith spoke up. "Don't do that. Snakes are carnivorous—they don't eat corn chips."

Tammy glanced over. "You heard her," she said sharply. "Don't feed the snakes." As Rune rolled her eyes and popped the chip into her own mouth, Tammy turned to Faith with a grateful smile. "Good eye, Faith," she said. "It's good to know we have someone in our group who's so knowledgeable. Actually, that gives me a ripper idea—are you free this evening after dinner?"

Faith glanced at Oscar. "I don't know," she said. "Oscar and I talked earlier about going sightseeing or something . . ."

"Let's reschedule that, babe." Oscar yawned. "Too tired. Think I might just go check e-mail with the others, then hit the sack early."

"Great!" Tammy said brightly. "Then, Faith, if you don't mind, would you like to help me take care of the snakes tonight?" She waved a hand toward the tanks. "I only know the basics myself, and unfortunately the fellow who's supposed to come in and do it got detained and won't be able to make it tonight after all."

"Sure, I'd be happy to help," Faith said immediately. Even after putting in her picketing duty, she couldn't help feeling a bit uncomfortable about having accepted such an expensive trip to Australia. This could be her chance to pay Tammy back, at least a little. Once again it meant delaying her serious talk with Oscar, but maybe that wasn't such a big deal. He already seemed to have forgotten about their fight. Maybe she should just try to do the same.

Oscar and the others left soon after that, leaving Faith and Tammy alone in the lab. The two of them worked companionably for a while, cleaning cages, misting the snakes that needed it, and doing other basic maintenance on the tanks and equipment. As they worked, Faith found herself telling the older woman a little more about her relationship with Oscar, as well as her latest thoughts about Arreglo.

Tammy listened sympathetically, nodding occasionally. "You need to follow your heart, Faith," she said when she'd finished. "I'm no fan of Arreglo's, as you know. But I think you should make things right with him if you want to, no matter what Oscar thinks about it."

"Really?" Faith said, surprised at how relieved she felt

to hear that. It wasn't as if she needed anyone's permission, exactly. But it was nice to have the approval of someone like Tammy.

"In fact, why wait until you get home?" Tammy went on. "I'm sure you could reach him at the conference if you want to. You could call his hotel first thing tomorrow."

"Oh, I don't know," Faith said, feeling shy at the very thought. "Now that I've worked it out in my mind, I don't mind waiting until we get home. I don't want to bother him when he's so busy."

"Hmm." Tammy seemed as if she might comment further, but suddenly changed the subject instead. "Hey, Faith, I just remembered something else I wanted to ask you. By chance do you know how to milk a snake?"

Faith nodded, knowing that Tammy was referring to the method of extracting a snake's venom. "Sure," she said. "I've done it lots of times."

"Well, remember that guy who was supposed to work here tonight? Guess what—he was also supposed to milk three of our snakes so the venom would be ready for our researchers tomorrow morning. And if we fall behind on the schedule . . ."

"Say no more. I'd be happy to help." Faith smiled. "Just show me who you need done."

Tammy pointed out the lab's two Common Brown Snakes and a medium-sized taipan. Then she moved off to sweep the floor, and Faith got to work.

As she carefully held one of the snakes by the head, forcing its fangs through a piece of clear latex stretched over the top of a glass container, Faith thought with some amusement that most people probably wouldn't think this was the greatest way to spend an evening while on vacation in Australia. But the truth was, she was having a better time than she'd had since arriving. It was nice to feel useful for a change.

13

"HEY, THERE! IT'S FAITH, right? Do you have a minute? We could use some help over there."

Faith glanced up to see Boone walking toward her. She took one more step out of the jungle into the sun. "Um, sure," she said. "What do you need me to do?"

Boone pointed down the beach. "We're trying to clear away some of the wreckage. Is your friend George around? We could use some more muscle power."

She didn't bother to tell him that she and George didn't exactly seem to be friends at the moment. "I—I haven't seen him in a little while," she said carefully. That was technically true; she hadn't seen him since leaving him to his vindictive snake hunt back in the clearing some fifteen or twenty minutes earlier.

"Oh well." Boone shrugged, squinting toward a small

group of people wandering down by the water. "Why don't you go help Locke move the small stuff? I'll go try to drum up some more help."

"Locke?"

"Bald guy. Cut around his eye."

"Oh! Okay." Faith knew exactly who he meant. It had to be the older guy she'd noticed staring out to sea, walking in the surf by himself, and generally standing a bit apart from the group much of the time. When she thought about it, she realized he did have a distinctive mark running vertically along the right side of his face, seeming to bisect his eye. Somehow it seemed to suit him, and she'd barely thought of it as a cut.

She found Locke sorting through some metal shards and other wreckage. When she introduced herself, he nodded and gazed at her silently for a moment. "This is quite a spot, isn't it?" he said at last.

For a moment she thought he was referring to the wreckage-strewn piece of beach where they were standing. Then she saw his eyes flicker briefly past her toward the jungle. She was about to nod politely and leave it at that. But something about the man's quiet intensity inspired her to answer more honestly.

"Yeah," she said shyly. "I mean, it's pretty scary to be here, with the crash and—you know, other stuff. But this place is gorgeous. So much natural beauty . . ."

"Indeed," Locke replied, going back to his work. "I've never seen anything like it. The jungle is filled with life."

Faith nodded. "I've seen tons of wildlife out there—lizards, spiders, snakes . . ." She smiled bashfully. "Snakes are kind of my thing. I'm a biologist—a herpetologist, actually."

"A natural scientist?" Locke looked interested. "You could turn out to be a very useful person to have around if we find ourselves stranded here for a while."

"Oh, I don't know about that," Faith demurred quickly. "I'm sure we'll be rescued soon. Besides, I probably wouldn't be as useful as you think—I'm just an academic; I don't know that much useful stuff."

Locke smiled, making the gash around his eye crinkle. "Any kind of knowledge can be useful, Faith. The only trick is knowing how to apply it."

Faith smiled back at him. "That sounds like something my sister might have said."

"Your sister must be a wise person."

"She—she was." Faith swallowed hard. "She's dead now. Cancer."

Locke paused in what he was doing, shooting her an incomprehensible look. "Sorry," he said at last. "I know how hard it is to lose one's family."

They worked in silence for a few minutes. Faith was picking metal shards out of the sand when the words slipped out of her on impulse—"Have you ever heard of the Paradise Parrot?"

Locke glanced at her. "Sure, I've heard of it," he said. "It's been extinct for decades. Why do you ask?"

"Um, you're right." Faith was already sorry she'd brought it up, but now that she'd started she figured she might as well finish. "It's extinct. At least it's supposed to be . . . I thought I saw one in the jungle yesterday, and again today. It was probably just a similar species, though," she added hastily. "We're all dehydrated, and I was probably just imagining things."

"Don't be too quick to dismiss what you see around here," Locke told her somberly. Then he smiled at her, his whole face seeming to rearrange with the change in expression. "You have an interest in birds, too, then? Not just snakes?"

Relieved that he didn't seem to think she was crazy, Faith laughed. "Sure," she said. "One of my earliest memories is going bird-watching in the backyard with my sister. Anyway, I love all animals . . ."

After that, the conversation moved along easily between them. Locke was surprisingly easy to talk to—unlike most nonbiologists she encountered, he seemed genuinely interested in what she had to say.

They were discussing extinction patterns a few minutes later when George emerged from the jungle nearby. He wandered toward them, shooting her a slightly sheepish look.

Locke noticed him, too. "Hello there," he called to George. "If you're not busy, Faith and I could use some help moving this big hunk of metal here." He rapped on a particularly large piece of wreckage.

"Sure thing," George said immediately, cracking his knuckles as he hurried toward them. "Where do you want it?"

He and Locke each took one end of the metal piece. At the count of three, they hoisted it up and moved it off to one side, revealing a cache of luggage that had been hidden underneath. After shooing away a few sand crabs that had taken up residence, Faith started opening the bags and sorting through the contents.

Meanwhile Locke and George carried the piece of wreckage away. As she worked, Faith watched them out of the corner of her eye, especially George. He was acting as if nothing unusual had happened between them, but she wasn't sure she could do the same. Thinking about the expression on his face as he'd grabbed that branch, the things he'd said, still made her feel upset and slightly nauseated.

When the two men returned, Faith cleared her throat. Normally she probably would have let things slide, brooded over George's behavior in private, and driven herself crazy. Somehow, though, just being on this island was making her feel a little braver. Maybe it was because after surviving that crash, a difficult conversation didn't seem quite as scary somehow.

"Um, George," she said softly. "About what happened out there in the jungle a little while ago . . ."

"What?" he said sharply, shooting her a wary look. "Nothing happened. Wasn't no big deal—not worth going on about."

"But those things you said . . ."

George barked out a short laugh. "Hey, I'm a hot-tempered guy," he said. "Sorry if I got a little carried away. I didn't mean to upset you, sweetheart. Really. You gotta ignore most of what I say, you know. I ain't that bright." Chortling at his own joke, he turned to Locke.

"Now little Faith here? She's quite the smarty-pants—getting her PhD and everything! Isn't that something?"

Faith bit her lip. She could tell George felt bad about what had happened before. She suspected he wanted to make it up to her without actually having to apologize. Or maybe he just didn't want to admit in front of Locke that he'd been terrified of a harmless little snake.

"Is that right." Locke smiled benignly. "So what is it you do back in the real world, George?"

"Real estate." George grunted as he hoisted another large chunk of metal. "Back home in Indiana, I buy up old farms or other unused land. Turn 'em into something useful by filling 'em up with brand-new subdivisions. Make a good living doing it, too."

It dawned on Faith that she'd had no idea what George did for a living back home. Now that she knew, it certainly explained his negative attitude toward her beliefs. His job could be considered the very antithesis of conservation.

"Interesting." Locke paused as he dug a large, hard-sided suitcase out of the sand. "That why you were in Australia, George? Business?"

"No, I was there for a personal matter." George frowned, staring down at the twisted piece of metal he was holding. For a long moment it seemed he wasn't going to explain further. Then he shrugged. "Hell, might as well tell you, seeing as how we're all stuck here together, right?" He sighed, his eyes suddenly taking on a distant expression. "I went over there trying to talk some sense into my daughter—she's just twenty-one, and dropped out of college to go live in Sydney with her tree-hugging know-it-all boyfriend." He glanced at Faith. "She looks a little like you—same build and hair color."

"Oh." Faith wasn't sure what to say to that. The more George said, the less she realized she'd known about him up until now.

George sighed again loudly. "She was gonna be the first one in the family to get her degree. . . . Could have maybe ended up a smart girl with a fancy title behind her name just like you, sweetheart." He smiled rather wistfully at Faith, then turned away with a grimace. "Anyway, sorry for going on about it. It just eats me up that she won't listen to reason, you know? Thinks she can do better on her own without any help from Dear Old Dad."

"No man is an island, entire of itself," Locke said as he dug through the suitcase he'd uncovered. "John Donne said that."

George stared at him as if he'd just sprouted an extra head. "Is that right?" he said. "Sounds like something my daughter might say, actually. She loves quotin' all that highbrow stuff, too."

His tone was sarcastic, and Faith cringed, wondering if Locke would take offense. Instead he just stared into the suitcase in front of him. "Well, look at what I just found," he said mildly. He pulled out a rectangular case.

"Is that a backgammon set?" Faith asked.

"Sure is." Locke seemed pleased. He shook the sand off the exterior and snapped it open, setting it down on the sand. Bending down, he poked through the plastic pieces tucked neatly into the built-in side compartments. "Looks like everything's still intact."

"That's cool." Faith was a little distracted by George, who was glowering toward the ocean with a faraway look on his face. "Should be a nice way to pass the time until we get rescued. Keep our minds working."

George glanced at them. "Right," he muttered sourly. "Should be a barrel of fun for the intellectual types around here—you know, the ones who care more about the lives of cockroaches and tree frogs than they do about people . . ."

The words hit Faith like an electric shock to her heart. What was he trying to say, anyway? Maybe he was still thinking about his daughter . . . but then again, maybe not. Her heart started beating faster, and she was filled with the uneasy sense that George had figured her out; somehow he knew what she'd done.

Impossible, she reminded herself. *Nobody knows. At least not anybody around here.* . . . Still the guilt bubbled up inside her, hot and bitter.

"Be right back," George said, hoisting another piece of wreckage onto one shoulder.

Trying to forget what he'd said, Faith stared across the beach. Her eyes gradually focused on a tall, slim figure approaching. It was the high-cheekboned woman.

"Hi. I'm Kate." She shaded her eyes with one hand as she stopped in front of Faith and Locke. "You guys have been sorting out the luggage, right? I need a backpack. Something light but strong."

"Backpack?" Faith stared at her blankly, still half-lost in her own thoughts. "Why?"

Kate looked a little surprised to be questioned. "We're going on a hike," she said. "Sayid and I."

That didn't seem like much of an answer to Faith. Who went on a hike at a time like this? But she couldn't quite seem to make herself care enough to inquire any further. If Kate and Sayid wanted to take their chances on missing the rescue plane because they were jaunting through the jungle, it was their own problem.

"Backpacks, hmm?" Locke replied, stroking his chin thoughtfully as he glanced around. "You've come to the right place. I just unloaded a couple that should do the trick." He picked up a couple of nylon backpacks from the pile of empty bags. "Take your pick."

"I'll take them both." Kate reached for the packs. "Sayid could probably use one, too. Thanks."

"So where are you off to on this hike of yours?" Locke asked her.

Kate answered him—something about a transceiver and finding a signal—but Faith's attention had already slid back to her own problems. She was still angry at George for the things he'd said and done, but the more she thought about it, the angrier she got with herself as well. As Gayle had always reminded her, you couldn't control other people. Only yourself. So why did she feel herself slipping into old patterns no matter what she did? What was wrong with her?

"Hey, are you okay?"

"Huh?" Faith blinked, realizing that Kate was staring at her with a concerned expression.

"You look kind of pale." The other woman shrugged. "Maybe you should get out of the sun for a while?"

"Um—maybe." Faith forced a smile. "Thanks."

"Sure. Bye." Kate hurried off again, backpacks in hand.

Faith hardly noticed. Her mind was churning, and she wasn't sure she was ever going to feel normal again. She wasn't even sure she deserved to feel normal . . .

"Want to play a game?"

She'd almost forgotten Locke was still there. "Excuse me?"

Locke looked up from his position crouched beside the backgammon set. "Game? I think we've done enough here to deserve a little rest." He didn't seem to notice her consternation, even though she was sure it was as clear on her face as that vertical scar was on his. Was he truly clueless, or just being polite? Faith was too upset to know, or even to care much.

"I don't think so," she blurted out. "I—I think she was right—I probably need to get out of the sun for a while. I think I'll go take another look for that bird I saw."

"Be careful out there," Locke replied. "And Faith?"

"Yes?"

"I hope you find what you're looking for."

14

". . . AND SO YOU SEE, *Faith, it's very important that the one thing works with the other thing and the third thing plays an integral part. Then all the little birds can fly away home. That's just the way of the world." Dr. Arreglo smiled broadly at her. "I'm sure you understand."*

"No, I don't!" Faith struggled to follow what her adviser was saying. But the more he tried to explain why he'd chosen to support Q Corp's plans, the less sense it made to her. Why couldn't she understand? She wanted to understand . . .

Suddenly a bird flew in the window and landed on Arreglo's desk. It was a species Faith had never seen before, a pretty little parakeet. Fluttering its colorful wings, it let out a chirp and then spoke to her in a familiar voice.

LARGER-PRINT BOOKS!

GET 2 FREE LARGER-PRINT NOVELS PLUS
2 FREE GIFTS!

HARLEQUIN®

Romance

From the Heart, For the Heart

LARGER-PRINT BOOKS!

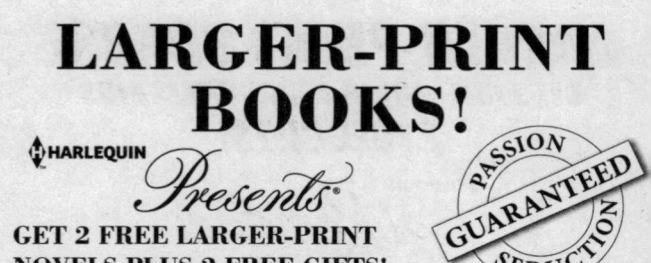

HARLEQUIN

Presents®

GET 2 FREE LARGER-PRINT NOVELS PLUS 2 FREE GIFTS!

PASSION
GUARANTEED
SEDUCTION

YES! Please send me 2 FREE LARGER-PRINT Harlequin Presents® novels and my 2 FREE gifts (gifts are worth about $10). After receiving them, if I don't wish to receive any more books, I can return the shipping statement marked "cancel." If I don't cancel, I will receive 6 brand-new novels every month and be billed just $5.30 per book in the U.S. or $5.74 per book in Canada. That's a saving of at least 12% off the cover price! It's quite a bargain! Shipping and handling is just 50¢ per book in the U.S. and 75¢ per book in Canada.* I understand that accepting the 2 free books and gifts places me under no obligation to buy anything. I can always return a shipment and cancel at any time. Even if I never buy another book, the two free books and gifts are mine to keep forever.

176/376 HDN GHVY

Name	(PLEASE PRINT)	
Address		Apt. #
City	State/Prov.	Zip/Postal Code

Signature (if under 18, a parent or guardian must sign)

Mail to the **Reader Service:**
IN U.S.A.: P.O. Box 1867, Buffalo, NY 14240-1867
IN CANADA: P.O. Box 609, Fort Erie, Ontario L2A 5X3

**Are you a subscriber to Harlequin Presents® books
and want to receive the larger-print edition?
Call 1-800-873-8635 today or visit us at www.ReaderService.com.**

* Terms and prices subject to change without notice. Prices do not include applicable taxes. Sales tax applicable in N.Y. Canadian residents will be charged applicable taxes. Offer not valid in Quebec. This offer is limited to one order per household. Not valid for current subscribers to Harlequin Presents Larger-Print books. All orders subject to credit approval. Credit or debit balances in a customer's account(s) may be offset by any other outstanding balance owed by or to the customer. Please allow 4 to 6 weeks for delivery. Offer available while quantities last.

Your Privacy—The Reader Service is committed to protecting your privacy. Our Privacy Policy is available online at www.ReaderService.com or upon request from the Reader Service.

We make a portion of our mailing list available to reputable third parties that offer products we believe may interest you. If you prefer that we not exchange your name with third parties, or if you wish to clarify or modify your communication preferences, please visit us at www.ReaderService.com/consumerschoice or write to us at Reader Service Preference Service, P.O. Box 9062, Buffalo, NY 14240-9062. Include your complete name and address.

HPLP15

"It's okay, Faithie. You don't have to understand everything. You just have to know who you can trust."

"Gayle?" Faith's heart pounded faster as she recognized her sister's voice. When she looked closer, she saw something of her sister looking out at her through the little bird's eyes. *"Is that really you?"*

The bird let out a melodic, twittering laugh. *"Of course it's me, sweetie! You knew I would never leave you all alone, didn't you? That's why I came back. Now we can be together again—a family."*

"Oh, Gayle!" Faith could hardly speak around the lump in her throat. *"I've missed you so much . . ."*

"Faith," Dr. Arreglo spoke up sternly. *"Your sister is right. You must figure out whom to trust, or all is lost."*

"Don't listen to him, babe!" Suddenly Oscar burst into the room, his eyes wild and angry. *"He's lying to you. His type always lies. How stupid do you have to be? He probably tricked you into thinking that bird is talking to you, too."*

"No, Oscar!" Now that Gayle was back, suddenly everything made perfect sense. Faith knew exactly how to reconcile Oscar's views with Arreglo's so that everybody would be happy. *"Please, just listen . . ."*

"The time for listening is past." Oscar stepped closer, his eyes blacker and narrower than ever. *"It's time for action."*

In the blink of an eye, his skinny limbs melded together . . . and in place of her boyfriend she saw a large tiger snake. Before she could react, it slithered up onto *the desk and sank its fangs into the bird-Gayle. The little creature struggled for a moment, a weak chirp emerging from its tiny beak. Then it went still.*

Faith tried to scream as the Oscar-snake turned its beady eyes toward her, but her throat spasmed like a writhing snake, and nothing came out . . .

"Faith! Yo, wake up, babe!"

Opening her eyes, Faith stared groggily up at Oscar, who was sitting on the edge of the hotel bed shaking her by the shoulder. "Whu—huh?" she mumbled as the remnants of her nightmare drifted away like mist.

"Wake up," Oscar repeated. "It's getting late. Besides, I just came in from getting us some coffee and there was a note at the front desk. For you. I thought you should see it right away."

Faith pushed herself to a sitting position, rubbing her eyes sleepily and wondering if she was still asleep and dreaming. Who would leave her a message at the hotel desk?

"Is it from Tammy?" she asked with a sudden flash of alarm, wondering if something had gone wrong with one of the snakes.

"Here, see for yourself."

He handed her the note. Yawning, she leaned forward and took it from him.

She came wide awake as soon as she saw the brief message scrawled on the scrap of hotel stationery. The handwriting was bold and distinctive—and very familiar.

Dear Faith,

    I received your message. I would like to talk with you ASAP—I do hope we can work things out—you have been one of the most promising students I've had the pleasure of knowing.

    If you can, please come to my suite this morning at ten. I have a few hours free at that time, so we will be able to talk privately for as long as you like. I'll give my people your name—they will let you through. I look forward to seeing you.

Yours sincerely,
L. Arreglo

Faith just stared at the signature for a moment, stunned. For a second she wondered if this was some kind of weird joke. But no—she had seen Arreglo's handwriting often enough to be certain that he had written the note himself. When she lifted the paper closer to her face to examine it, it even smelled faintly of his aftershave.

So the note was real. But what was he talking about? She hadn't left him any messages . . .

Suddenly noticing that Oscar was gazing at her with a sheepish grin, she stared back at him suspiciously. "What?"

"What do you mean, 'what'?" he replied playfully.

She frowned and pushed back the sheets, swinging her legs over the edge of the bed. "Look, it's too early for games," she said. "Just tell me what you know about this note, and why you look like the cat who swallowed the canary, okay?"

He held up his hands in a gesture of surrender. "Okay, okay, you caught me," he said lightly. "I, um, might have left a note for Arreglo at his hotel."

"Might have?"

"Okay, *did,*" he admitted. "I called it over there and had his hotel staff transcribe it so the handwriting wouldn't give me away—I wanted him to think it really came from you."

Faith put one hand to her forehead. Her mind still felt a little fuzzy with sleep, and she was having trouble following his story. "But why?" she asked. "What did you say to him?"

He shrugged, letting one hand fall onto her knee. "I felt kind of guilty, you know?" he said. "Putting so much pressure on you—I know you, like, still admire the bast—er, I mean Dr. Arreglo. It wasn't right of me to try to turn you against him and stuff."

"Really?" she said cautiously, waiting for the punch line. Was she still asleep and dreaming? This didn't sound much like the Oscar she knew at all.

"Really," he assured her with a laugh, giving her knee a squeeze. "You don't have to look so surprised, babe. I want to do whatever I can to help you reconcile with him—if that's what you want, it's what I want. I just want you to be happy."

"So you sent him a note telling him I wanted to talk with him . . ." she said slowly, still trying to wrap her mind around what he was saying.

Now that she was slowly starting to catch up to what had happened, the thought of what Oscar had done made her a little uneasy. Sending a note like that wasn't at all something she would do—and she really wasn't sure it was his place to do it for her, especially without checking with her first. He was so impulsive. . . . What if he'd decided to send an insulting note instead, something that would ruin her relationship with Arreglo once and for all?

But he didn't, she reminded herself, her worry gradually starting to be overtaken by gratitude. As surprising as it was, Oscar had put aside his hostility toward Arreglo—just to make her happy. Whether she would have handled things the same way or not, she was touched by the gesture. It had been a long time since anyone had done something so selfless for her. A very long time . . .

I guess he really does care about me, she thought with a shiver. It felt good to know that she was no longer alone in the world.

15

IT FELT GOOD TO be alone as Faith trekked into the jungle. Even though the crash had only happened about twenty-four hours earlier, give or take, she was already growing weary of living in a crowd of strangers. It wasn't that most of the people weren't perfectly nice; in fact, she was surprised at how much she already liked several of them—Locke, Claire, Hurley. . . . It was just that she was used to spending much of her time alone, or with one or two carefully chosen companions. As a child she'd wondered if there was something wrong with her for not liking big parties or other crowded events. But she'd grown to accept that it was just the way she was made—sort of like a snake, preferring a more solitary existence most of the time. After a day in the company of others, she just needed to get away from everyone for a while.

Especially George.

She bit her lip as she remembered what he'd said. Had she overreacted? Gayle had always said she was as sensitive as a canary in a coal mine, often seeing criticism where none was intended . . .

Crack!

Snapping back to attention, Faith stopped short and glanced around warily. The noise had come from somewhere up ahead and to the left, though she could see nothing moving in the thicket of vines up there. She'd been in such a hurry to get away that she'd almost forgotten her earlier fear of being alone in the jungle, but now it all came flooding back. Her heart started to beat a little faster and her palms felt clammy. How far was she from the beach, anyway?

Taking another few steps, she held her breath and listened. The hairs prickled on the back of her neck, giving her the eerie feeling that she was being watched. She tried to convince herself that that was silly—she was a good distance away from camp, and there was no sign that any of her fellow castaways had ever come this way. Still, she walked a little faster, her eyes darting from side to side. The jungle was full of movement, as usual—small brown birds hopped from branch to branch overhead, calling cheerily to one another; the breeze tickled the fronds of a cluster of squat palms nearby; just ahead a lizard scurried out of sight with a flick of its long, whiplike tail.

It should have been an idyllic, soothing scene. Normally Faith would have loved the freedom of being alone with nature in such a beautiful setting. But no matter how she tried to convince herself otherwise, something about this place just didn't feel normal. Maybe it wasn't safe out there; maybe she should head back right now and . . .

A sudden flash of color just ahead distracted her from her thoughts. She gasped, her eyes trying to focus on the small blur of turquoise and red, pale green and dark brown. She stepped forward into a sunbeam so intense that for a second she was almost blinded. Staggering through it, she blinked rapidly, trying to follow the movement of the bird hopping along the leaf-littered ground just ahead, jumping from one puddle of dappled shade to another. If she could only get a closer look at it, at least she would know . . .

Her foot came down on a dry twig, setting off a sharp retort that echoed through the jungle. With a flurry of feathers the bird took off, darting between tree trunks, its long tail flicking up and down as it flew with an undulating motion.

"Wait!" Faith blurted out, breaking into a run. She dashed in the direction the bird had gone, fearing that she'd lost it again already. But as she rounded a rocky outcropping, she caught another glimpse of the turquoise feathers just above its tail before the bird disappeared again into the shadows.

She raced after it, keeping her eyes trained straight ahead. As she passed through a small bamboo grove, the rustling of the dry, narrow leaves seemed to harmonize with her panting breath. Emerging on the other side of the grove, she almost ran straight into a cluster of heavy vines hanging down from an ancient tree. Skirting around it, she paused for a moment, breathing hard as she scanned the area around her for the parrot.

There was a flicker of movement in a bush just ahead. Faith barely caught a glimpse of the bird before it took off again, flying fast and low to the ground. She took off after it again, jumping fallen logs and rocks and doing her best to avoid getting snagged or snapped in the face by branches and undergrowth. The humid air was still and close, and she could taste her own sweat and feel it stinging her eyes. Running alternately through bright sunlit clearings and dense shade made her feel a little dizzy, but she didn't dare slow down. She didn't want to lose the bird again.

As she started to wonder how much longer she could keep up her pace, the parrot abruptly changed course, veering downhill and to the right through a sunny, hilly wash dotted with enormous boulders. Faith skidded after it, trying to keep upright on the shifting, rocky footing. Just when she thought she'd lost her quarry yet again she saw it dead ahead. It was perched on a long, straight branch in the shade of a large overhang, its head bobbing slightly.

Finally! Faith crept forward, her heart in her throat. All she had to do was keep quiet, and she would have the answers she needed. If only she could make a positive ID, could confirm that there was indeed a living example of *Psephotus pulcherrimus* sitting on that branch just ahead, she knew it would make everything bad that had happened over the past couple of days seem a little less disastrous. It might even mean that landing here in this jungle really did have a purpose . . .

Squinting, she stepped carefully toward the bird. Its bright lime-green chest seemed to glow out of the dimness of the shady overhang, but in the sharp contrast between light and dark, her eyes had trouble making out any other details. She had to get closer . . .

At her next step a rock twisted out from beneath her foot, sending her falling heavily to her knees. Pebbles and larger stones went skittering noisily down the hillside. Startled, the bird flew up and over the scrubby trees in the wash, disappearing back into the jungle.

"No!" Faith cried out in frustration, her words bouncing back at her from the edges of the wash. "Come back . . ."

Picking her way across the rest of the wash as quickly as she could, she jogged into the jungle in the direction the bird had gone. There was no sign of it, so she picked a direction at random. Moving as quickly as she could in the dense underbrush, she scanned the treetops in vain. It was only when she tripped on a tree root and almost fell flat on her face for the third or fourth time that she knew it was time to give up. The bird was gone.

Sighing with frustration, her toe throbbing from where she'd tripped, Faith glanced around . . . and suddenly realized she had absolutely no idea where she was. The excitement of the chase wore off quickly, replaced by fear. She was lost.

Looking around, she tried to hold down her panic.

This wasn't the first time she'd found herself off course in the wilderness—all she had to do was stay calm and re-trace her steps. But she was only able to follow her own prints for a few yards before they were lost in the deep leaf litter on the jungle floor. She was surrounded by a forest of tall, weird-looking, smooth-barked trees with enormous clusters of dangling air roots. The under-growth here was sparse, making it impossible to trace her path through broken branches or other signs. Glancing up, she realized she couldn't even see the sun through the dense tree canopy to get a sense of which direction she should head in to get back to the beach.

She wandered aimlessly for a while trying to get her bearings. The humid air seemed to breathe with her, mak-ing her feel claustrophobic and panicky. Why had she run off willy-nilly like that? It wasn't like her to be so impul-sive and thoughtless. Somehow, though, catching up to that bird had seemed like the most important thing in the world—for a moment it had made her forget all her fears and anxiety, all the problems of the past couple of days. Now here she was, without what she'd been after, and even worse off than before. So much for acting on im-pulse. What was she going to do now?

After a few minutes she stopped in a clearing, trying to fight back the panic welling up inside her. She looked around, willing herself to stay calm and think things through, figure out a way to get herself out of her predicament. Stately, gnarled trees surrounded the clear-ing, their thick leaves far overhead blocking her view of the sun and casting gloomy shade over the area. Vines

dangled here and there like long, lifeless fingers stretching toward the earth. The ground was covered with a carpet of two-foot-tall, pale-green grass that undulated
slightly as a breeze glided through the clearing.

Or *was* it a breeze making the grass move that way?
Faith's palms went clammy as she suddenly noticed that
the movement was confined to one area—the thin blades
tipped and swayed exactly as if brushed aside by a large,
unseen snake slithering toward her.

Taking a step backward, Faith glanced around nervously. Another section of the grass started to sway and
bend. Then another. And another.

She spun wildly in a circle, sudden dread gripping her
throat and making it hard to breathe. The movement was
everywhere. She was surrounded! The jungle around the
clearing had gone oddly silent, and she could hear the
faint *sssh, sssh* sound of scaly bellies brushing along the
ground.

Even in the midst of her growing fear, a small part of
her mind rebelled against what was happening. Snakes—
it was only snakes. Staring at the circle of motion, she
tried to convince herself that it was silly to panic. She
loved snakes. She understood them; she had devoted her
life to them.

But that didn't change the fact that now, for the first
time in her life, she found herself utterly terrified of
them . . .

A bird cried out from somewhere just above her head,
startling her. She glanced up. There was no sign of the

bird that had called, but she noticed one of the thick, fingerlike vines hanging down just over her head

Her eyes darted back to the ground. The unseen serpents were only a few feet away now, coming fast from all directions. They would reach her in seconds.

Jumping straight up, she grabbed the vine and held on tightly, swinging her legs up and out of the grass. She didn't dare look down as she scrabbled for a higher handhold, her arm and shoulder muscles screaming in protest. Hand over hand, her breath coming in ragged gasps, she managed to drag herself upward. Once she was able to wrap her legs around the vine, climbing became a little easier. She didn't stop until she reached the refuge of a sturdy tree branch twenty feet off the ground. Pulling herself up onto it, she slid along it until she could lean against the rough bark of the trunk, her chest heaving as she tried to catch her breath.

When she looked down into the clearing, the grass was still.

16

FAITH SAT MOTIONLESS ON the edge of the bed staring at the note from Arreglo. Her mind was filled with half-formed questions, and she wasn't sure what to think or say or do next.

"Well?" Oscar spoke up, a touch of impatience in his voice. "Are you going to meet with him, or what?"

"Um, I don't know. I guess it would probably be better to wait until we get back home and he's not so busy . . ."

"Don't be ridiculous," Oscar said immediately, grabbing the note from her and waving it in her face. "He wants to see you—even set aside some time. It would be, like, rude not to go."

"Oh." She hadn't thought of it that way. "Maybe you're right. I'm not even sure how I'd get in touch to say

I wasn't coming. . . . Oh! I don't even know how to get to his hotel! How am I going to—"

"Relax," he interrupted before she could spin into a full-blown panic. "I'm the one who called him, remember? I know exactly where he's staying and how to get there. I'll take you there—but you'd better hurry up and get dressed! We don't have much time."

Her eyes darting to the clock on the bedside table, Faith realized he was right. She'd slept later than she'd thought; it was already nearly nine o'clock.

Leaping out of bed, she scrabbled through the dresser drawers where she'd unpacked her clothes. She was glad she'd brought her nicest nubby tweed skirt and the pale green blouse that looked almost like real silk.

"Be right back," she told Oscar as she scurried for the bathroom.

The water in the hotel shower heated up right away, unlike that in either the ancient bathtub in her dorm room back home or the cramped shower stall at Oscar's apartment. She stood under the stream for a long moment letting the water wash the rest of the sleep-fuzzies from her mind. Even then, it all still didn't feel quite real—the note, the appointment to see Arreglo—but she didn't have enough time to worry about it much.

When she emerged from the shower, she heard a low murmur from the room outside. For a moment she thought Oscar had turned on the TV, but then she heard him laugh and realized he had to be talking on the phone.

Vaguely assuming he'd called Tammy or one of the

others, she quickly dried herself off and grabbed her toothbrush from amongst the jumble of Oscar's toiletries on the countertop. She was beginning to think she'd underestimated him—she never could have predicted that he would react this way to the current situation. She smiled at herself in the mirror through a froth of toothpaste, realizing that just as Arreglo was the one who'd brought them together in the first place, he was now bringing them closer than ever. It almost made Faith start to believe in fate . . .

Oscar's voice had been quiet at first. But as she turned off the water after brushing her teeth, she heard his words coming louder and faster. He always got that way when he was excited, and she listened fondly, vaguely wondering what he was talking about.

". . . *mumble mumble* . . . I told you it would work. It's on!" he said sharply. "It's totally on."

As he lowered his voice again, she reached for the clothes she'd draped over the closed toilet lid. She realized the skirt she was holding was the one she'd been wearing during her first meeting ever with Dr. Arreglo, well over a year ago now. The thought made her stomach flip over nervously, just as it had done that day. Could she and Arreglo really get their relationship back on track? When she thought back to their last conversation, it seemed almost impossible. But his note made it sound not just possible, but likely . . .

"Yes!" Oscar's voice rang out clearly from the other room, breaking into her thoughts. "I told you I'm up for it, and I am. Don't worry. I can do this—trust me. In fact, I can't wait."

He sounded almost angry, and she shot a glance toward the door with concern. His voice had already dropped back to mumbling volume, and even when she stepped closer to the door, she couldn't hear what he was saying.

Then her gaze fell on her wristwatch, which she'd set on the countertop. Seeing the time, she forgot about Oscar's conversation and hurriedly finished dressing. She was so nervous that she felt physically ill, but she clung to the idea that Arreglo wanted to see her. If she could make things right between them, it could end up being one of the best things to come out of this trip.

One of the lines from his radio speech popped into her head: *One can't have an influence if one isn't willing to engage.* It could be seen as an excuse for selling out one's values—or a tribute to the potential and power of compromise. Maybe even Oscar would someday come to understand that.

"Faith?" There was a knock at the bathroom door. "Almost ready, babe? We need to go."

"Coming." Quickly running a comb through her damp hair, Faith gave herself one last glance in the mirror and then hurried out to join him.

Oscar was standing in the narrow hallway outside the bathroom, tapping one foot. He was wearing a wide-brimmed hat she'd never seen before, and had Faith's blue nylon windbreaker slung over one arm.

"I probably won't need that," Faith told him, nodding

toward the jacket. "Not if it's as warm out as it was yesterday. Where'd you get that hat?"

"Better put it on anyway," Oscar said, ignoring her question. "It'll be air-conditioned at Arreglo's hotel, and your hair's still wet."

Touched by his concern, she shrugged on the jacket despite the clammy heat of their room. She was still surprised by how supportive he was being about this. Following him down the hall outside, she gazed at him with a new sense of wonder, admiring the determined set of his jaw as he punched the elevator button several times.

"What?" he demanded, noticing her stare.

"Nothing," she said shyly. "I'm just kind of impressed that you're being so cool about this, writing that note and everything. . . . You know—because of how much you hate Dr. Arreglo."

He shrugged and shot her a little half smile. "Hey, I'm full of surprises." He laughed, grabbing her and giving her a quick squeeze. "Seriously though, babe, your happiness is more important to me than anything else." Letting go, he jiggled his weight from foot to foot and glanced up at the elevator indicator. "How long does it take to get an elevator in a freakin' six-story building?"

Faith ducked her head to hide a smile. It was obvious that he was feeling tense. It couldn't be easy for him, knowing he was doing something nice for his sworn enemy, Arreglo. She promised herself that she'd figure out a way to pay him back for this later.

"Finally!" Oscar snapped as the elevator doors slid open at last. "Come on, babe. We gotta hurry . . ."

Fifteen minutes later they were walking into the hushed, elegant lobby of a high-dollar hotel. Even in her best clothes, Faith felt a little out of place among the fashionably dressed men and women standing at the concierge desk or browsing through the magazines in the spacious sitting area. She pulled her windbreaker closer around herself and glanced around nervously.

"Ready to head upstairs?" Oscar asked.

She noticed that he'd just pulled out a pair of mirrored sunglasses and put them on. "Why are you wearing those in here?"

He grinned and yanked the brim of his hat a little lower. "Cut me a break, babe," he said. "I want to be here to support you and all. But I don't want any of my friends seeing me hanging out with Arreglo." He laughed loudly, causing a few people to turn and glance at him curiously.

"Very funny." Faith smiled nervously. "But listen, I'm okay from here. You don't have to come upstairs with me—maybe you could wait in the coffee shop or something . . ."

"No way!" Oscar said immediately. "I want to be with you—you know, for moral support. I figure I owe you after being such a jerk about this before. Please?"

Faith hesitated. She really wasn't sure it was a good idea to take Oscar up to meet Arreglo. What if he couldn't resist saying something obnoxious once they were face-to-face?

Seeing the doubt in her face, Oscar grabbed both her hands and gazed at her over the top of his sunglasses. "Seriously, beautiful," he said. "I want to prove that I'll do anything for you. You're my world, you know."

She still melted a little every time he called her "beautiful." Besides, maybe she wasn't quite ready to face Arreglo alone anyway.

Squeezing his hands, she nodded gratefully. "Thanks," she said. "It's almost ten—guess we'd better head upstairs and get this over with."

17

FAITH'S ARMS ACHED AS she lowered herself to the jungle floor. Even though there was no sign of any snakes in the grass anymore, she'd clambered through the branches of the large tree until she could climb down well beyond the edges of the clearing.

As she rubbed her raw, sore palms on her shorts, she was already starting to feel foolish. She glanced toward the grassy clearing, which looked serene and beautiful beyond the edging of trees. Even if those had been snakes back there, she wasn't sure what had made her panic like that.

Or maybe she was. Those snakes hadn't just been going about their business; she knew it as certainly as she knew her own name. They had been stalking her. And snakes just didn't *do* that . . .

"Aaaaaaaaaaaaaah!"

The shout of terror was faint, but instantly recognizable even at that distance.

"George," Faith whispered as the echoes of the cry rang through the forest.

She stared off in the direction from which the shout had come. For a second she was tempted to ignore it. Surely there was someone closer who would go to his rescue this time. Besides, he was probably just afraid because he'd seen a particularly scary beetle crawl past on the jungle floor . . .

"Help! Help me, someone—please!"

She couldn't do it. She couldn't ignore a cry for help— not even after all the things George had said and done. She couldn't make herself not care about him, one human being to another. It was the same softheartedness that had made her stop to rescue an injured robin when she was late for an interview as a teenager. It had almost cost her the job, but she still hadn't been able to regret it—especially when she and Gayle had released the fully healed bird from the roof of their apartment building and watched together as it soared up into the sky, joyful and free . . .

She hurried through the jungle, adjusting her route as necessary each time George cried out again. It occurred to her that following his voice was also almost certainly leading her back toward camp. She was glad about that, though distracted by trying to follow the sporadic cries.

After a while, as the cries grew louder and closer, she

realized she was back on familiar ground—she recognized the oddly twisted branch of a particular tree from an earlier stroll, and that distinctive rock formation over there. . . . A moment later she swore she could smell the salt spray from the beach.

Her relief was soon overshadowed by another cry: "Help! Please! I—I can't stay here much longer!"

Hurrying forward, she found herself at the edge of an open, rocky area. Enormous boulders studded the ground here and there, while at the far end the rocky ground rose steeply into a jagged cliff topped with a row of palms that leaned out over the drop-off as if peering over the edge at the ground far below.

George was balanced on his left hand and both knees on a narrow spit of rock near the bottom of the cliff. It was some four feet off the ground, about the size and shape of a surfboard, and lined on both sides by thick, thorny bushes. His right hand clutched a small, battered-looking valise, and she guessed that he'd just retrieved it from among the roots and stones just above where he was perched—she could see a few other pieces of debris from the plane up there. At the moment he was looking down at the rock in front of him, his teeth gritted, though whether with fear or pain she wasn't sure.

At first she had no idea what was going on. Were his clothes or skin caught in the prickly bushes? Or had he perhaps fallen from farther up the cliff, injuring his back? What if he was paralyzed? She would have to find her way back to the beach, find Jack . . .

After a second she realized it wasn't doing George any good for her to stand there in a panic and speculate. "Hello!" she called to him, her voice shaking a little. "George? What are you doing up there?"

His head whipped around immediately. "Faith!" he gasped out, sounding relieved to see her. "Thank God. Tell me this is another one of those harmless little baby pythons, all right?"

It was only then that she saw the snake. Coiled on the rock just two feet in front of George, its head swayed back and forth menacingly as it stared at him.

Faith's heart skipped a beat. Not wanting to jump to any conclusions, she took a few steps forward. Only a few yards away now, she had an unobstructed view of the snake's short but thick body, broad, triangular head, banded brown and gray scales, and thin, yellowish tail tip. She stared at it for a moment, trying to convince herself that she had to be mistaken about what it was.

"Well?" George demanded anxiously. His gaze had left Faith and returned to the snake. The two of them, man and serpent, seemed to be trying to stare each other down. "Is it safe to move?"

"No!" Faith blurted out. The snake heard her; it shifted slightly, its tongue flickering and its tail switching slightly as it sought the source of the new voice. She did her best to keep her voice calm and soothing, not wanting to rile the snake any further. "George, you're going to have to stay very still. That's an *Acanthophis*."

"A what?" George's voice held an edge of irritation,

along with panic. "Talk English, okay? Is this thing poisonous?"

"Yes." She swallowed hard as the snake let out an ominous hiss. "Very. It's more commonly known as a Death Adder."

18

WHEN THE ELEVATOR DOORS hissed open, Faith was surprised to see several burly uniformed men standing in the hallway a few doors down. "What's going on?" she whispered nervously to Oscar.

He glanced down the hall. "Bodyguards," he said. "Arreglo's not exactly Mr. Popular with everyone these days, remember?"

Faith stared out through the elevator door, suddenly feeling ambivalent about this whole adventure. Why hadn't she trusted her first instinct to wait until she got home to deal with this? Being here just made everything so much more complicated.

"Maybe this wasn't such a good idea," she mumbled.

Oscar let out an impatient snort. "You can't chicken out now, babe," he said. "Come on—let's go."

When Faith still didn't move, he gave her a forceful shove. She stumbled forward, catching her balance in the hallway outside just as the elevator doors started to close behind her. Oscar jumped out after her in the nick of time.

She shot him an irritated glance. "Why'd you push me?" she said. "You know, the more I think about this, the more I think maybe we need to sit down and have a good talk, and soon. I'm starting to feel like you've been making more and more of my decisions lately—including this whole trip, come to think of it—and I'm not really sure I like it. That's not the kind of relationship I thought we had."

He shot her an edgy grin that didn't quite seem to reach his eyes, which were darting here and there along the hall. "Sorry, baby," he said. "Whatever you say. We'll talk about it later if you want. If it still seems important then, anyway."

She narrowed her eyes at him, not sure what he meant by that last part. Before she could ask, the bodyguards spotted them.

"You there," one of them called out in a booming voice. "Can I help you?"

Faith gulped, intimidated by the man's sheer bulk as well as his businesslike demeanor. She found herself staring at the name tag on his chest, which read TIM J., NEW SOUTH WALES SECURITY SERVICE.

"Um . . . I'm Faith Harrington?" she squeaked. "I'm— that is—um . . ."

"She's here to see Arreglo," Oscar finished for her, grabbing her arm and dragging her forward a few steps.

The guard gazed at him with a hint of suspicion. "Harrington," he said. "Yeah, Arreglo said he's expecting her. Who are you?"

"I'm with her." Oscar tilted his head toward Faith. "Boyfriend."

"That's right," Faith added quickly. "I invited him along. I hope that's okay." She could tell the guards were just doing their job, being cautious. But she hated to think what might happen if their suspicious questions and stares triggered Oscar's temper. She wasn't sure she could deal with the fallout of one of his rude, offended outbursts at the moment.

Two of the guards exchanged a look. Then the first one, Tim J., shrugged. "S'pose that's all right, then," he said. "Afraid we'll have to frisk you, though, mate. You understand."

Faith winced, anticipating the howl of outrage that was certain to follow. Oscar hated submitting to any sort of authority figure—back home, he tended to jaywalk on purpose if there was a cop around, and he always paid his rent on the final hour of the final day before the cutoff because his landlord had once hassled him about paying at the last minute.

To her surprise, though, he immediately stepped forward and spread out both arms. "Frisk away, my good man," he said jovially. "Nothing to hide here."

Faith stared at him in surprise as the guard expertly ran his hands over Oscar from top to bottom. "Okay. You're clean, mate," he said. "Go ahead." He nodded toward the door behind him.

"Thanks, mate," Oscar said, stepping forward and rapping sharply on the door.

Faith realized she was sweating. She slipped off her windbreaker and clutched it tightly in front of her, wishing she had a few more minutes to compose herself. This had all happened so fast that her head was still spinning, and she realized she hadn't had so much as a cup of coffee since being so abruptly awakened. No, she definitely wasn't sure she was ready to face Arreglo just yet.

"Want me to hold that for you, babe?" Oscar asked, grabbing her jacket and slinging it over his arm before she could answer.

"Thanks." She rubbed her hands together apprehensively. "I don't really know why I'm so nervous . . ."

Oscar grabbed one of her hands and squeezed it so tightly his fingernails dug into her skin. "Don't be. You'll be great," he assured her. "Great. This is going to be great . . ."

Just then the door swung open, filled with Arreglo's smiling, bearded mass. "Faith, my dear!" he cried, his eyes lighting up with joy. "You came—I am so happy to see you!"

Suddenly, just like that, it all seemed a lot easier. Why had she been so nervous? Looking into his caring eyes and open face, Faith immediately felt much better. More comfortable. She knew it still wouldn't be easy to say some of the things that needed to be said, or reconcile some of their new beliefs, but now at least she was sure it would be worth it to have Arreglo back in her life. He was the only father figure she'd had in a long time, and she'd hardly even realized how much she'd missed him. She found herself glad now that Oscar had been so pushy, both figuratively and literally. Otherwise she might never have summoned up the courage to come.

"Hi," she said softly. "I—I came to say I'm sorry . . ."

Arreglo shot a wary glance at the guards, then a curious one at Oscar, before returning his attention to her. "Me, too, Faith," he said kindly. "Me, too. But come—let's go inside and talk." He leaned out past her to speak to the guards. "My friends, I really need to talk to dear Faith here," he told them. "Please don't allow anyone to disturb me until it is time for my next meeting." He turned and winked at Faith. "That gives us a couple of hours to work things through, all right? I hope that will be enough."

Faith smiled and allowed Arreglo to usher her and Oscar through the door. She waited while he closed it behind them, then followed him down a narrow hallway that had to be nearly thirty feet long. At the end of it was a thick wooden door, and beyond that, the space opened up into a spacious, airy sitting room. One wall was a solid sheet of glass offering a soaring view of downtown Sydney a dozen stories below. A small but comfortable-looking bedroom was visible through a half-open door in another wall. The furnishings were modern and luxurious, and large potted palms nodded at them from the corners of the room.

"This is nice," Faith said politely as Arreglo stopped in the middle of the room.

"Yes—I normally wouldn't stay somewhere quite so

fancy," Arreglo said, stroking his beard and looking around. "But Q Corp insisted on sponsoring my trip here, and so here I am."

Faith shot a quick, anxious look at Oscar, certain that he wouldn't be able to let that one slide. But he hardly seemed to be paying attention as he fiddled with her jacket, shaking it out and laying it on a sleek black leather chair. He'd also removed his hat and sunglasses, setting them on the seat of the same chair.

"And speaking of the devil, as most of us have always regarded Q Corp"—Arreglo let out a short laugh—"I want to assure you, Faith, that I will do my best to explain why I did what I did. I know it made you very upset, and I can understand why."

"It just surprised me, I guess," Faith said shyly. "I—I probably overreacted. But it seemed like such a change for you, and that kind of freaked me out. I don't really like sudden changes, I guess."

Arreglo nodded and smiled. "We shall talk it all through," he said. "I want to try to help you understand my motives a little better. I think when you hear everything, you will see that I made the better choice. Even if you don't agree, I think it will make more sense, you know? I'm just so glad you're here—I felt terrible about what happened between us."

"Okay. Thanks." Faith smiled at him, feeling as if a weight was being slowly but surely winched up off her heart. Finally, her world seemed to be moving back to normal . . .

Suddenly realizing she hadn't introduced Oscar, she turned to him with a smile. He was standing back a bit, his hands in the pockets of his baggy khaki pants.

"So sorry, Dr. Arreglo," she said. "I forgot you haven't met my boyfriend, Oscar Wolfe. Oscar, come meet Dr. Arreglo."

"Welcome, my son," Arreglo said, stepping toward him and extending his hand. "Any friend of Faith's is a friend of mine."

"It's a pleasure to meet you, sir." Oscar pulled his right hand out of his pocket, grasping the older man's hand and shaking it heartily. "I brought you a little gift . . ."

Oscar was still shaking Arreglo's hand as his own left hand emerged from his pocket. It was holding something cylindrical and shiny. *Is that a syringe?* Faith wondered with confusion. *What is he—*

Before she could finish the thought, Oscar yanked Arreglo toward him and plunged the syringe into the man's chest.

19

FAITH FELT HER HEART pounding in her chest as she stared at the snake, trying to figure out what to do. "Stay still," she called to George as she saw him shift his weight from one knee to another.

He let out a groan. "Don't know if I can," he said. "Not for much longer anyway . . ."

Faith bit her lip, willing her sluggish mind to think. Death Adders weren't as fearful of humans as some other species, so it wasn't very likely that the snake would decide to retreat on its own if it hadn't already done so. However, the species had also been found to be less likely to strike unless actually touched. That was probably why George had been able to get away with shouting and shifting his weight and everything else so far. She didn't want to put any money on things continuing that way, though. If George had disturbed the snake's resting place, it might be irritated enough to strike out at him if he made any sudden moves.

"Stay still," she called again.

"You said that already." He sounded breathless and anxious. "So what am I supposed to do? I can't stay in this position forever."

Focusing her gaze on him, she saw that he was right. The narrow spit of rock on which he was perched was only a little wider than his body, making it nearly impossible for him to shift his position. The uneven rock was also still dotted with puddles from the earlier rainstorm, which had to make it even more difficult for George to keep his balance. The sheer cliff wall was only inches behind him; the spiky thorns of the bushes inches away on either side; the snake just a couple of feet in front of him. His normally ruddy face was white with exhaustion and fear.

If I hadn't turned up when I did . . . , Faith thought, though she didn't bother to finish the sentence. So far, aside from identifying the snake, her arrival hadn't done him much good.

"Okay, just hold tight for another few seconds," she called as reassuringly as she could, hoping his knees and balance could hold out for a little bit longer. "I'm going to get you out of there."

"Hurry," he said through gritted teeth. He stared at the snake, which swayed slightly and flicked its tongue at him.

Tearing her gaze away from the pair of them, Faith cast a desperate glance around the clearing. She had already considered and rejected the idea of throwing something at the snake to distract or kill it. Even if she thought her aim was up to the task—which she most certainly didn't—she was afraid that might only make things worse. A distracted snake was more likely to strike out at anything around, and if she hit it but didn't kill or disable it, that would only irritate it further.

Luckily she had already hit on another plan, one much more likely to work. "Just hang on . . ." she said distractedly, walking toward the edge of the forest and scanning the ground.

"What are you doing?" George's voice took on a panicky edge as she moved out of his line of sight. "Don't leave me here!"

"I'm still right here," Faith called to him. "I'm not leaving. I'm just looking for a . . . aha!" Suddenly she spotted exactly what she needed.

Hurrying forward a few steps, she picked it up. It was a fallen branch, about three feet long and an inch or so around. More importantly, it ended in a V shape, its twin prongs each an inch or two long.

As she moved back into his line of sight, George squinted at her anxiously. "What's that?" he demanded. "You're going to need a bigger stick than that if you're going to kill this thing."

"I'm not planning to kill it," Faith replied calmly, moving forward toward George's rocky platform as smoothly and carefully as she could. She didn't want the snake to hear her coming and panic. "I'm going to use this forked stick to trap it. If I can get it just behind the head, it won't be able to move its head enough to bite you, and you'll be able to step over it safely."

"What?" George sounded incredulous. "Give me a break, girl. Just find a big rock and smash the thing to kingdom come!"

"No, that's not necessary. This will work."

George glared at her. "Not necessary? It sounds like you care more about protecting the damn snake than saving my life! What's wrong with you?"

Faith took a deep breath, doing her best to ignore his rather insulting tone. "That's not true," she told him. "This is the best way. It's safer, and nothing has to get killed."

George barked out a short, bitter laugh. "Oh, man. This just takes the cake, don't it? You environmental types always think you know best . . ." He shifted his weight, raising his shoulders slightly and sending a couple of pebbles bouncing down to the ground. "I've got a better plan, sweetheart. You make some noise—beat that dinky little stick of yours against a tree or something—so the snake gets distracted. Then I'll jump up and kick it away before it can bite me."

"No!" Faith blurted out, alarmed. "You can't do that. If we get the snake too riled up it's likely to go after either or both of us!"

"Not if I get to it first," George muttered, gripping the

handle of the valise even more tightly. Despite his bold words, though, he suddenly seemed a lot less excited about trying his "plan."

Faith sighed, so frustrated by his foolish bluster that she was ready to give up. Maybe it would be better to run to the beach for reinforcements. George might be more likely to listen to someone like Jack—a man, a natural leader, someone he respected . . .

At that moment George's knee slid out from under him by a few inches, sending a few more pebbles skittering off the edge of the rock shelf. George caught his balance, but the Death Adder tensed and raised its head. Freezing in place once again, George stared at the snake with terror in his eyes.

Faith gulped. There was no time to run for help. George was too scared and too impulsive by nature; if she left, she suspected he was quite likely to try something stupid just to put an end to the terrifying standoff. It was almost a miracle that it hadn't already happened. She had to be strong, to stay and try to help him, no matter what happened. If he panicked and did something foolish anyway? Well, she would just have to deal with it.

"Okay, listen to me," she told George briskly, trying to copy his own businesslike tone as best she could. "We're going to do this my way. You need to stay as still as you can until I give the word, okay? Don't move, or try to get up and smash the snake with that suitcase, or anything else. If it bites one of us . . ." She grimaced slightly as the relevant statistics flooded her mind. "Let's just say that without access to antivenin, our chances wouldn't be that great."

"Whatever," he muttered, seeming mesmerized as he gazed at the snake.

She hesitated, watching him for a second or two. Could he do it? Would he stay still and calm until she gave the word, or would he panic and doom himself, and quite possibly her, too, to a nasty and painful death from snakebite? He clearly didn't trust her or her plan. Could she trust him?

There was only one way to find out. She gripped the forked stick tightly and crept forward . . .

20

ARREGLO STAGGERED BACKWARD, CLUTCHING his chest. His face registered surprise, confusion, and pain. His mouth opened, but no sound came out—just a small bubble of saliva that hung on his lower lip for a moment. The syringe came loose and clattered to the floor.

Faith gasped in horror as Arreglo's legs collapsed and he crumpled to the ground, his head bouncing painfully off the sharp edge of the modern coffee table. "Oscar!" she cried. "What did you—"

With three swift steps, Oscar was at her side. He grabbed her, covering her mouth with a hand. "Not a sound," he murmured in her ear. "We totally lucked out with this crazy hotel suite—those guards outside shouldn't hear a thing. Not unless you do something stupid, like scream."

Her eyes wide, Faith shook her head. She wasn't a screamer anyway—Oscar knew that. When she got really scared, her voice shut down, and the most she ever managed was a startled squeak.

Oscar loosened his hold on her mouth. "Promise? No screaming?"

She nodded, and he released her. She immediately dropped to her knees at Arreglo's side. His eyes were rolled back in his head, and his chest heaved, his breathing coming in quick, ragged gasps. He appeared to be unconscious.

"What did you do?" Faith exclaimed, still not really comprehending what was happening. "Oscar, what—"

"Haven't you figured it out yet?" Oscar sounded pleased with himself and almost cheerful. "I thought you were supposed to be so smart, Ms. PhD."

Faith's gaze turned to the syringe, which was lying beside Arreglo's shoulder. A small trickle of blood was pooling beside it, soaking into the pale fibers of the hotel carpet. "What was in that thing?"

"Snake venom." Oscar grinned proudly. "Pretty appropriate, don't you think?" He shrugged. "Well, okay, there was some superfast-acting tranq in there, too—didn't want him fighting back or making a lot of noise while the venom did its thing, you know."

Faith blinked. None of this was making sense to her. "But where did you get . . . ? Why . . . ?" Feeling her mind start to go numb with shock, she shook it off. This was no time to panic. "Never mind," she said. "We have to help him! What kind of snake did the venom come from? We need to get some antivenin and—"

"No." He put a hand on her shoulder and squeezed firmly, stopping her before she could get up and rush to the door. "Wait. You can't go out there—what do you think is going to happen to you if people come in here and see this?" He waved one hand at Arreglo, who was still gasping for air like a beached fish.

"What are you talking about?" Faith cried, her grasp on reality starting to slip a little. This was all too much—nothing in her life had prepared her for such a situation. For a second she had the eerie, unbalanced feeling that she was acting out a scene in a movie or something. "Oscar, I still don't understand what's going on!"

Oscar sighed, sounding more like his usual impatient self. "Get with the program, babe," he said. "You can't really be this dense, can you? Do you really think the IAL would pay all those expensive overseas plane tickets just so we could wave a few signs? No way—*this* is why we're here." Once again he indicated Arreglo. "The IAL wants to send a message to anyone who might decide it's a good idea to compromise with Big Bad Business. We've been planning this since the day Arreglo made his big announcement."

Faith put her hands to her ears, not wanting to hear any more. None of this made sense; none of it. She wasn't the type of person who got involved in these sorts of things—she didn't even like reading about them in the newspaper. And Oscar. . . . She stared at him, wondering if she really knew him at all.

She tried to breathe in and out to stave off the panic, but the air got stuck in her throat. In front of her, Arreglo's body twitched and he let out a deep groan.

Oscar leaned down and grabbed the syringe, holding it up to the light. Faith could see that there was still some liquid sloshing around inside. "Oops, guess I didn't get it all into him." Oscar shrugged and glanced down at Arreglo. "Looks like it was more than enough to do the trick, though." After sliding a keeper onto the end of the needle, he tucked the syringe into his pants pocket.

As the unconscious Arreglo struggled to breathe, Faith struggled to keep her wits about her. She was very aware of the seconds ticking by—seconds that might be crucial in saving Arreglo's life. Somehow, though, she couldn't seem to make herself act or think or do anything but kneel there staring in horror.

Oscar was still talking. "Okay, now we've got to get out of here," he said, grabbing her windbreaker and shoving it at her. "Just follow my lead, and don't do anything stupid. Those hired goons outside know I couldn't have smuggled in that syringe—they checked me over pretty good, remember? So when they find out about this, they'll know it had to be you." He smirked, picking up his sunglasses and sliding them on. "Just keep that in mind as we're leaving, babe."

"But I didn't—," she started to protest, then gasped, remembering how she'd noticed Oscar fiddling with her jacket after they came into the suite. "You put it in my pocket, didn't you?" she accused, feeling the truth of it like a punch in the gut. "You made sure I wore my jacket because you knew they probably wouldn't frisk me."

"Bingo." Oscar grinned as he slapped his hat on his head, pushing it down so it covered most of his forehead. "Now you're starting to catch on!" He grabbed her by the arm, dragging her to her feet. "Now come on, let's get while the getting's good. We need to be far away from here before someone finds him."

Faith's mind was crying out against everything that was happening. It seemed to be frozen in the moment before Arreglo had extended his hand to Oscar, as if refusing to accept anything that had happened after that. If only reality could work that way, with some sort of cosmic rewind button. . . . She stood frozen in place, staring down at Arreglo. Oscar must have pumped a huge dose of venom into him. Maybe it was already too late to help him.

"Come on!" Oscar sounded really impatient by this time. "What are you waiting for? In case you don't realize it yet, you're a wanted woman now."

That broke through the fog a little. "Me?" she cried. "But I didn't do anything wrong!"

Oscar laughed. "Hey, that may be true," he said. "But who's going to believe it? As far as anyone outside this room will know, you're an accomplice. You were the one who got us access to Arreglo, you were the one who smuggled in the venom—hell, you were even the one who got some of the venom out of the snakes, remember?"

Faith closed her eyes, flashing back to the extractions she'd performed the previous evening at the lab. She'd thought she was doing it to further the cause of cancer research. Instead . . .

Oscar wasn't finished. "Besides, who will be there to bail you out of jail and help you find a decent lawyer?" he taunted, peering at her over the top of his glasses. "Nobody, that's who. I'm all you've got, babe."

His words seemed somehow crueler than anything else he'd done so far. Oscar knew she had no living family—no one to count on in a bad situation except herself. Arreglo had been the person who'd come closest in the past few years, and then Oscar himself, of course, or so she'd thought. Besides them, there was nobody else. Not anymore.

Feeling her whole world crumbling around her, she didn't resist as Oscar grabbed her arm and hustled her toward the door. She walked passively down the long interior passageway and stopped in front of the outside door.

"Remember, just play along," he hissed warningly in her ear.

Then he swung open the door. The guards, who had been slouched against the walls, immediately snapped to attention.

"Anything wrong, mate?" one of them asked. "You're, uh, back sooner than we thought."

Oscar's chuckle sounded surprisingly normal. "Don't worry, guys," he said with a playful wink. "I won't tell the boss you were slacking off." He tilted his head toward Faith. "No, the little lady here just started feeling sick— she's afraid of heights, and the big windows in there freaked her out, I guess."

"Sorry to hear that, miss," the guard said, smiling at Faith.

"Anyway, Dr. Arreglo asked us to give you a message on our way out," Oscar continued, his voice still light and casual. "He wants to take a nap before his next meeting. So he said you should still keep anyone from disturbing him until it's time to get ready for that. Okay?"

"No worries." The guard shrugged agreeably. "He's the boss, right?"

"Right!" Oscar laughed again, then gave the guard a friendly slap on the shoulder. "See you guys around, okay?"

Tightening his hold on Faith's arm, he steered her down the hall to the elevator. The doors slid open only seconds after he punched the button, and he gave her a gentle shove to propel her inside the empty car.

She turned around to face the front, her feet shuffling as slowly as an elderly woman's. Then she stared blankly ahead as the doors slid shut.

21

GEORGE'S EYES WERE WIDE and wild with fear as he stared down at the Death Adder. After giving him one last anxious glance, Faith turned her attention to the snake. She carefully judged the distance left between her and the edge of the rock shelf, then took a few careful steps forward. She was still worried about all the impulsive and stupid moves George might possibly make, but she was doing her best to push such thoughts out of her mind. She needed to focus and do what she had to do, come what may.

"Easy," she murmured, though she wasn't really sure whether she was talking to George, the snake, or herself. She figured it was probably a little of each. "Easy, now . . ."

Taking one more step, and then another, Faith eased forward until she was only about three feet from the front edge of the rock shelf. Due to its gradual slope from front to back, the front end was a little lower than she'd thought initially; the top was about even with her waist. Clutching her stick in both hands, she raised it to shoulder height and took one more step.

She was within striking range now. The Death Adder was still watching George, seeming unaware of or uninterested in her approach.

Faith paused, her stick held at the ready, wondering if she could really do this. Though she had a healthy respect for it, the snake itself didn't scare her much—she had handled much worse in the past. What made her mouth go dry and her whole body tremble was the thought of what might happen if she failed. The possibilities flashed through her mind in full Technicolor. She could miss, the stick could break or skid off the rock . . .

It would be bad enough if the snake turned on her—thanks to her background, she knew exactly what she would have to look forward to if that happened. But if it struck out at George, perhaps sank its fangs into his face or neck, she wasn't sure she could handle the guilt. It would mean another death on her conscience due to a bad decision. . . . For an endless second, it seemed better just to stand there, frozen in time, and do nothing rather than risk the possibilities.

Just then a colorful little parakeet-type bird flashed by, warbling tunefully, and snapped Faith out of her inertia.

Blinking gratefully up at the bird as it disappeared from view, she then returned her attention to the task before her. She still wasn't sure if she could trust George not to do something foolish. But that didn't matter. It was far more important to trust herself. After all, that was the only thing she could control. The old Faith might not have believed that. But now she did.

Not giving herself a second chance to freeze, she lunged forward, jabbing the stick firmly down against the rock. The snake thrashed—once, twice, three times—flinging its body around so violently that for a terrifying second she couldn't tell if she'd failed or succeeded.

Then it stilled for a moment before thrashing again, giving her the chance to see that she'd done it—the snake's large, triangular head was being held firmly against the rock, trapped neatly between the branches of the fork at the end of the stick. She pressed down as hard as she dared. She didn't want her hands to tremble and let the stick slip, but at the same time she didn't want to push so hard that the branch snapped in two. It was a balancing act, a careful compromise between too much and too little.

"Now!" she called urgently to George, who remained frozen in place. "Go! Climb over it and keep going."

But George still didn't move. What was he waiting for? Ripping her gaze away from the snake just long enough to glance at him, Faith saw that his eyes were fixed on the struggling serpent and his face was drained of all color.

"Oh, no," she whispered.

Her lunge and the snake's violent thrashings must have overwhelmed whatever bravado he'd had left. It was clear that he was too terrified to move—even to save himself. Now what was she supposed to do?

"George?" she said tentatively. "Hey, George! Snap out of it, okay?"

He didn't respond or move at all. She swallowed hard, being careful not to let up the pressure on her stick. The snake's thick body flung itself from side to side, smacking her soundly on the arms and torso, but she barely felt the pain. She was frozen with indecision once again, trying to decide how to deal with this completely unanticipated turn of events.

But this time she didn't allow herself to freak out. Glancing down at the rocky ground, she spotted an oval-shaped rock beside her right foot. It was about the size of an elongated grapefruit and solid—more than heavy enough to smash in the head of the Death Adder. It would be easy enough to stoop down and scoop it up while still keeping one hand on the stick. It would be even easier to use it to kill the snake while she had it trapped and helpless.

The thought made her feel queasy in the pit of her stomach. Why should this snake die for George's cowardice? Her hands on the stick trembled as she remembered the pretty little spider he'd killed without a second thought. Then there were the countless creatures that must have been displaced by his developments back home—birds, reptiles, rabbits, deer, insects, spiders, fish, and many more. What about them? Had he spared even a momentary pang of pity or guilt over them? Had he thought about them at all?

She knew what Oscar would say she should do . . .

"I'm not Oscar," she muttered fiercely, shaking her head as if to banish the memory of him. She *did* care about the snake, it was true. But she cared about George as well. Even after all that had happened. He was still a fellow human being.

Glancing down, she reached out with her toes and shifted the rock a little closer. It was there if she needed it—and she knew she would use it if she had to. She was strong enough to do what was necessary to save George's life.

But she was also strong enough not to give up on her ideals just because the going got tough. She still believed in compromise, so first she wanted to see if there might be another way . . .

22

"LOOK, I TOLD YOU. No compromise, no backing down." Oscar sounded smug as he pushed the hotel room door shut behind them. "Whatever it takes—survival of the fittest, baby."

Faith couldn't believe that Oscar was standing there arguing with her as if they were merely disagreeing over what to order for dinner or who to support in the next election. As if he hadn't just killed a man . . .

She barely remembered leaving Arreglo's suite, or walking through his hotel lobby, or the cab ride back to their own hotel. But now that they were in their own room, her mind was starting to break out of its deep freeze, at least a little bit. She walked toward the bed on numb legs, stunned by the enormity of what had just happened. Lowering herself carefully into a sitting position on the edge of the mattress, she felt her heart thumping violently and tears threatening to spill over. Her head hurt, her stomach hurt, and her heart hurt—she almost wished she could go back into her numb, painless daze for a while.

"This can't be happening," she insisted desperately. "Oscar, please tell me what's really going on here, okay? Because I just don't get it."

She stared at him, hoping against hope that something he might say would help her understand. That he would offer up some explanation, some information that would help her mind make sense of the crazy thing that had just happened. That this could still turn out all right.

"I already told you." Oscar pulled the syringe out of his pocket and set it carefully on the dresser. "This was all exactly how it was supposed to go. We've been planning for this moment since before you and I met—it was, like, destiny." Kicking his shoes off, he flopped onto the bed.

Faith's brain seemed to be sputtering along like a cold car engine in subzero temperatures. Even so, she was slowly starting to make some connections that perhaps should have been obvious earlier.

"Wait," she said. "So you knew those other people before this trip? Mo, Rune, Junior . . ."

"Sure." He tossed his hat and glasses on the bed and glanced at her. "Mostly just online, of course. But we're all members of IAL from way back—only the most trusted people from the group were in on this plot, naturally."

"And when you and I met . . ." She struggled to understand. "You were just looking for someone who knew Ar-reglo? Someone who could get you access to him?"

"But you're much more than that now, baby." Oscar gave what she guessed was supposed to be a reassuring smile. "Not only were you absolutely perfect for the role, but you turned out to be quite the cool little girlfriend, too." He flopped onto the bed beside her, making the mattress bounce, and planted a sloppy kiss on her cheek. "That's why we changed the plan a little so maybe you wouldn't have to end up taking the fall."

Her entire body shuddered as she pushed him away. "Wait," she said again. "You guys were going to blame this whole thing on me?"

"Sure. It makes the most sense, doesn't it? But once I started spending time with you, I really started to dig you. You have potential—in fact, we were going to let you in on the whole plan if we thought you were ready." He shrugged. "Clearly you weren't, so we went with Plan C. Anyway, I know you'll come around after a while and see that this was the right thing to do. Then everything will be cool."

She shuddered again, horrified at how deeply and completely he'd misread her all this time they'd been to-gether. Didn't he know her at all? She had never been one to believe much in soul mates, but she'd thought that they at least understood each other a little. Now it seemed they'd just been seeing what they wanted to see—on both sides. As if they'd been coexisting on parallel but slightly different planes of reality all along.

"Anyway, what's done is done, right?" Oscar was already losing interest in the conversation. "The IAL is prepared to get us both new identities here in Oz so we can disappear—probably to Malaysia or somewhere—and never get caught. You turned out to be perfect for that part of the plan, too." He touched her gently on the nose. "Nobody's going to miss you or wonder too much where you are when you don't go back to school."

Even though she was pretty sure he wasn't trying to be cruel this time, Faith felt a stab in her heart at his comment. Anger bubbled up inside of her, hot and painful. She had never liked confrontation, but suddenly her soul was crying out for it. She wanted to leap at Oscar, grab him by the throat, scream at him until he was forced to understand exactly what he'd done . . .

Those feelings scared her, and she shot an involuntary glance at the window as if in hopes of some kind of escape. At that moment a pigeon fluttered gracefully in for a landing on the sill, distracting her slightly. She ran her eyes over its smooth, soft gray feathers as it did its slightly awkward bird-walk along the windowsill.

Think with your brain, not with your heart.

Her sister's words popped into her mind unbidden, as they often did during difficult moments in her life. How many times had Gayle said that to her, usually when it was too late to follow her advice?

But it wasn't too late this time—not entirely. Her heart pounded as Faith realized she had to make Gayle's words a reality, right here and now. Despite the almost overwhelming mixture of betrayal, horror, sadness, and humiliation that made her want to burst into sobs of fury and smash Oscar's face in, she had to keep her cool if she wanted to get through this. Oscar had just showed her how ruthless he could be, and he was clearly more than a little nuts. If he thought she might turn him in or otherwise cause trouble with his precious plan, there was no telling what he would do. She needed to handle him as carefully as she would an agitated rattler coiled to strike.

Realizing he was watching her carefully, she put a hand to her forehead. "I—I need to take this all in," she said weakly, pretending to be confused. That wasn't much of an acting challenge, considering that she was still feeling dazed and not entirely sure any of this was actually happening. "It's all just so sudden, I—I may need some time to get used to it . . ."

"Take all the time you need, babe." Oscar's face lit up, and he grabbed her knee and squeezed it. "I'm here for you. You'll see—we'll get through this together, and it will be great."

"Thanks." She forced a smile, carefully keeping her voice as normal as she could. Out of the corner of her eye, she was suddenly all too aware of the syringe of snake venom on the dresser just a few feet away. "Um, I think I need to go wash my face," she said. "Okay?"

"Go for it." Oscar leaped up and gave a little bow, all his movements eager and excited.

Faith stood, willing her rubbery legs not to collapse under her. Choked with fear, she walked carefully toward the bathroom. When she reached the dresser she paused for a split second beside the syringe, then kept going without reaching for it. Instead she continued on into the bathroom.

She felt a little safer just being around the corner and out of Oscar's sight. Leaving the door ajar to avoid any chance of raising his suspicions, she ran the water in the sink and splashed her face. The cool water felt good against her flushed skin and cleared her head a little. Plus the activity bought her a moment to think about what to do next.

Oscar's voice drifted in from the room outside. "You won't regret it if you stick with me, baby," he called. "We're in this together, and that's how it should be. We're a team now. Forever."

There's no such thing as forever.

That was something Gayle had said a lot toward the end. Lifting her head, Faith stared at herself in the mirror. Her wide amber eyes, so much like her sister's, stared back at her, but didn't tell her what to do.

When Faith emerged from the bathroom, Oscar was sitting on the corner of the bed with his back to her as he dug through his suitcase, which was flung open on the floor at his feet. Once again she paused beside the syringe. All she had to do was grab it—she could jab the needle into Oscar's neck or shoulder before he realized what she was doing. If the tranquilizer and the venom did their trick, nobody would find him until it was too late, and she was long gone.

But once again she turned away from the syringe. She couldn't do it. Not even in these circumstances, and not even to him.

Instead she grabbed the metal ice bucket from the dresser nearby. Acting fast before she could lose her nerve, she jumped forward—and brought the bucket down as hard as she could on the back of Oscar's head.

"Hey, I—" he blurted out, sounding surprised. Then he slumped like a marionette whose strings had just been cut, sliding off the edge of the bed and landing on top of his open suitcase with a thump.

Faith stood frozen for a moment, ice bucket in hand, staring down at him. His sides moved in and out, reassuring her that he was still alive. She was half-expecting him to leap up, shake off the blow, and come at her furiously. Then it would all be over . . .

But Oscar didn't move. Stunned by what she'd just done, she dropped the ice bucket on the bed and covered her mouth with both hands, willing herself not to throw up or faint. Then, realizing that time was still sliding along without her, she grabbed the phone, stepping over Oscar's prone form to reach it. Dialing with shaky fingers, she managed to get connected with the local police.

"H-hello?" she said, her voice squeaky and unrecognizable even to herself. "I need to report a crime. The environmental convention—someone needs to check on Dr. Arreglo immediately—don't let the security guards stop you. It's very important he get medical treatment as soon as possible. He was injected with snake venom, definitely from a toxic species, but I don't know which kind, so you'll need an ID kit or a polyvalent antivenin . . ." She didn't know if it was too late to save Arreglo or not. But she had to try.

"I see." The operator sounded surprised and perhaps slightly suspicious. "What's the victim's location?"

For one panicky moment, Faith couldn't recall the name of Arreglo's hotel. Then it popped back into her head, and she blurted out the name.

"All right," the operator said calmly. "Now your location, please, miss?"

The Faith who had always been a good girl, had always made her bed and done her homework and respected her elders, obediently opened her mouth to answer. But the new Faith, the person stuck in this strange game where she didn't know the rules but had to play anyway, came to her senses and took over just in time.

"Um, I'm . . . somewhere else," she stammered. "Now I have to go. Good-bye." She flung down the phone, feeling panicky, as if suspicious eyes were staring in the windows at her. Spinning around, she saw that the pigeon was watching her with its round black eyes. As she stared at it, it took off in a flurry of wings.

Faith flew into action as well. She yanked open the dresser drawers and started tossing her things into her carry-on bag as quickly as she could. Now that she'd done what she could to help Arreglo, all she could think about was getting far, far away from this place. Some vague part of her brain knew that it couldn't possibly end there, but she would have to deal with the rest of it later.

Somehow she found her way outside to a cab, and then to the airport. Hardly seeing the throngs of travelers going about their own business all around her, she found her way to the Oceanic Airlines counter. "I need to trade this in," she said to the woman there. "For an earlier flight."

The agent looked at her tickets. "I see," she said pleasantly. "So you're wanting to head back to the States a bit early, then?"

"Please," Faith said, trying to keep her voice as calm as possible. "I have to get home now—today. It's very important. Can I switch to a different flight?"

"I'll see what I can do."

The agent bent her head over her computer, her fingernails clicking rapidly across the keyboard. After a moment she looked up with a smile.

"As a matter of fact, it looks like we've just this moment had a cancellation on flight 815, which begins boarding in about fifteen minutes," she said. "Must be your lucky day."

23

FAITH TOOK A DEEP breath. "JUMP, YOU IDIOT!" she shouted at the top of her lungs.

Her words were so loud they made the nearby trees rattle as startled birds and other creatures jumped or flew off. It even startled her a little—it was very unlike her to make that much noise, ever.

But it worked. "Huh?" George grunted, breaking out of his silent, fearful stupor.

He abruptly scrambled forward, almost crashing into the stick Faith was holding. Just in time he lurched off to one side, slipping off the rock shelf and tumbling to the ground, catching his shirt on the edge of the pricker bush before landing heavily on his back.

"Oof." He lay there stunned for a second or two before

clambering awkwardly to his feet and rushing away across the clearing, tripping over rocks and roots in his haste.

Faith watched over her shoulder, still keeping a firm hold on her stick. She wanted to make sure he was safely out of range before she moved.

He finally stopped at the far end of the clearing, where he turned to look back. "Kill that evil thing!" he shouted hoarsely.

Faith stared at him. Then she glanced down at the rock by her foot. She kicked it away, sending it bouncing off into the shadow of some scrubby trees. Then, with one last deep breath, she released her grip on the stick and leaped away as fast as she could.

The snake let out an angry hiss, whipping around into striking position. But seeing nothing close enough to attack, it almost immediately turned and slithered rapidly across the rock shelf, disappearing into a fissure near the back.

Faith let out a breath she wasn't even aware she'd been holding. Just then she heard shouts from the jungle behind where George was standing. She turned just in time to see a small group of survivors emerging from the trees. Locke was leading the way, followed by Michael, Claire, and a couple of others whose names she didn't know.

"What happened?" Claire called out.

Michael hurried up to George. "We heard you guys yelling all the way at the beach. . . . Is someone hurt?"

Faith cringed in anticipation of what George would say: *She let a dangerous snake get away—she's crazy . . .*

But when she glanced over at him, he was smiling at her. "I'll tell you what happened," he told the others, his voice already returning to its usual booming tone. "This girl saved my life, that's what happened!"

Everyone talked at once, demanding more information. Only Locke was silent, rubbing his chin thoughtfully as his eyes wandered from Faith to George and back again. George was talking fast, quickly outlining for the others what had just happened.

"Nice work, Faith." Michael stepped forward to clap her on the back. "Very brave."

Claire nodded, shivering slightly. "Definitely brave," she declared. "I came across a Death Adder once while hiking out in the bush—they're totally scary!"

Finally George held up a hand for silence. "Listen, I want to say something." He turned toward Faith. "I was in a pretty bad spot there, and I don't know what might've happened if you hadn't come to my rescue. And after some of the things. . . . Well, let's just say I wouldn'ta blamed you for passing me by."

Faith blushed. In the background, Claire tittered slightly and a couple of the others exchanged glances.

George shrugged. "Anyway, I ain't much with the flowery words. So I'll just say thank you, Faith. You're a brave and honorable person—a good friend. I won't forget this." His eyes were sincere as he held out his hand.

"I—uh—you—" She was so surprised and touched that she wasn't sure how to answer. So she just took his hand and shook it.

As she pulled her hand away, she caught a glimpse of

bright feathers nearby. For a moment she thought it was the tiny parakeet that had flown by earlier, but when she glanced over, she saw a larger bird disappearing into the trees. Her heart thumped.

"Excuse me," she told George and the others hastily. "I'll be right back."

She raced off after the bird, tracking it as it zoomed along just above the forest floor. It led her through several patches of light and shade, around several rocky outcroppings, and along a narrow, winding stream. For a while it pulled so far ahead that she was sure it was going to get away again, and the thought nearly broke her heart.

But then, quite suddenly, she caught up to it in a small mossy clearing. It was perched on a rock, preening its colorful feathers.

Breathless, she stopped short and stared. The sun was shining down into the clearing, and she was finally able to see the bird clearly. It lifted its head and hopped down from its rock, jumping a few feet across the ground. With a chirp, it turned around and hopped back onto the rock again.

She stayed there for a while watching it. Then she heard a flutter from overhead, and looked up just in time to see a dozen nearly identical birds swoop down toward the clearing from the tree canopy. She gasped as they dropped to the ground like a shower of colorful jewels; her ears were filled with their melodious cries.

Soon she couldn't pick the original bird out of the group. The parrots hopped around on the ground for a moment, mingling and merging. Then, as if on some unheard signal, they took to the air all at once, smoothly and swiftly, like multiple parts of a larger organism. Their flapping wings filled the air as they rose high above the clearing, free and alive.

Smiling, Faith tipped her head up toward the sky, watching the birds fly off together. Somehow, all this time she'd pictured a single parrot living here in this jungle all alone. She was glad to see that that wasn't the case—but then again, she should have known it already. After all, nature didn't often leave her creatures all on their own.

As the last of the flock disappeared over the treetops, Faith heard footsteps approaching through the jungle. Glancing over her shoulder, she saw Locke coming toward her.

"Where's everybody else?" she asked him.

He nodded in the direction of the beach. "They took George back to camp," he said. "Figured they'd have Jack give him a once-over, just to be on the safe side."

"Oh." Faith turned her eyes back toward the sky, searching the endless blue expanse for one last glimpse of the birds. But they were gone, and despite her disappointment she couldn't stop smiling.

Locke followed her gaze. "Did you find what you were looking for?" he asked in a conversational tone.

She hesitated. "No," she replied at last. "Not really. That bird—um, it turned out to be nothing like I thought it was. I should have known that you can't just turn back time like that—get something back that you know is lost forever. . . . I feel kind of foolish for spending so much energy trying to chase it down."

Locke shook his head. "That's nothing to feel foolish about, Faith," he said. "A place like this—well, it can make people see what they want to see."

She turned and glanced at him. He was smiling at her, but his eyes seemed to be staring at something much farther away.

"Are you finished here?" he asked after a moment. "I'll walk you back to the beach if you like."

"Yes." She smiled and shot one last look at the sky. "I'm ready. Let's go."

The **must-have**
book for fans.

BONUS
DVD INSIDE
BEHIND THE SCENES OF LOST

LOST

THE OFFICIAL COMPANION BOOK

**Includes a detailed episode guide, behind-the-scenes looks
and back stories to help uncover the mysteries of *Lost*.**

Lost Season 2 Wednesdays 9/8c

GET LOST ON DVD

Over 8 Hours of Bonus Features

See *Lost* as you've never seen it before — presented in a widescreen theatrical format with 5.1 surround sound, and bursting with exclusive bonus features including unaired flashbacks — *Lost* on DVD is a real find. **Now On DVD**

LOST: The Official Magazine

The hottest show becomes the hottest magazine, as Titan Publishing Group launches *Lost: The Official Magazine!* This bi-monthly magazine features exclusive material all *Lost* addicts will be going primal to get hold of — leading you closer to the island's secrets!

For more informtion visit: titanmagazines.com